250 Yummy Quick and Easy Thanksgiving Recipes

(250 Yummy Quick and Easy Thanksgiving Recipes - Volume 1)

Victoria Morgan

Copyright: Published in the United States by Victoria Morgan/ © VICTORIA MORGAN

Published on September, 22 2020

All rights reserved. No part of this publication may be reproduced, stored in retrieval system, copied in any form or by any means, electronic, mechanical, photocopying, recording or otherwise transmitted without written permission from the publisher. Please do not participate in or encourage piracy of this material in any way. You must not circulate this book in any format. VICTORIA MORGAN does not control or direct users' actions and is not responsible for the information or content shared, harm and/or actions of the book readers.

In accordance with the U.S. Copyright Act of 1976, the scanning, uploading and electronic sharing of any part of this book without the permission of the publisher constitute unlawful piracy and theft of the author's intellectual property. If you would like to use material from the book (other than just simply for reviewing the book), prior permission must be obtained by contacting the author at author@rutabagarecipes.com

Thank you for your support of the author's rights.

Content

250 AWESOME QUICK AND EASY THANKSGIVING RECIPES 7

1. After Thanksgiving Casserole 7
2. Apple Cider Sweet Potatoes 7
3. Apple Oatmeal Bar Cookies 8
4. Apple Pudding 8
5. Apple Sausage Stuffing 8
6. Apple Walnut Salad 9
7. Apple And Pumpkin Dessert 9
8. Asparagus With Cranberries And Pine Nuts 10
9. Australian Style Pumpkin Scones 10
10. Autumn Apple Salad II 11
11. Autumn Stuffed Acorn Squash 11
12. Bacon Wrapped Pork Medallions 11
13. Bacon Wrapped Turkey Breast Stuffed With Spinach And Feta 12
14. Bacon And Almond Green Bean Casserole 13
15. Bacon Garlic Green Beans 13
16. Baked Acorn Squash With Apple Stuffing 14
17. Baked Corn Casserole 14
18. Balsamic Butternut Squash With Kale 14
19. Banana Pudding IV 15
20. Basic Corn Muffins 15
21. Basic Mashed Potatoes 16
22. Basic Yankee Bread Stuffing 16
23. Bernie's Big Batch "Apple Pie In A Jar" Jam 17
24. Best Ever Pecan Pie Bars 17
25. Black Friday Sandwich 18
26. Black Friday Turkey Salad 18
27. Blackberry Cobbler II 19
28. Blue Cheese And Pear Tartlets 19
29. Bourbon Glazed Carrots 19
30. Brie Cheese Pizza 20
31. Brie, Cranberries, And Pistachio Wreath .. 20
32. Broccoli Cheese Squares 21
33. Brown Sugar N' Bacon Green Beans 21
34. Brussels Sprout Slaw 22
35. Brussels Sprouts Gratin 22
36. Bulgur Wheat With Dried Cranberries 23
37. Butternut Squash Soup II 23
38. Butternut Squash And Pecan Casserole 23
39. Buttery Garlic Green Beans 24
40. Candied Apples II 24
41. Candied Apples III 25
42. Candied Sweet Potatoes 25
43. Caprese Appetizer 25
44. Carmel's Stuffing 26
45. Cheesy Broccoli Rice Casserole 26
46. Cheesy Mashed Potatoes With Cubed Ham 27
47. Chef John's Easy Apple Pie 27
48. Chef John's Perfect Mashed Potatoes 28
49. Chicken Or Turkey Pot Pie 28
50. Chinese Style Peanut Cookie 28
51. Chocolate Bar Hot Chocolate 29
52. Chocolate Pumpkin Bundt® Cake 29
53. Cindy's Turkey Salad 30
54. Classic Savory Deviled Eggs 30
55. Cozy Mulled Wine 30
56. Cranberry Apple Oatmeal 31
57. Cranberry Gravy 31
58. Cranberry Jalapeno Cream Cheese Dip 32
59. Cranberry Pecan Cake 32
60. Cranberry Stuffed Turkey Breasts 33
61. Cream Cheese Snowball Cookies 33
62. Cream Corn Like No Other 34
63. Creamy Pumpkin Spice Martini 34
64. Curried Carrot Soup 35
65. Deborah's Holiday Mashed Potatoes 35
66. Delicious Cinnamon Baked Apples 35
67. Delicious Vegan Hot Chocolate 36
68. Deviled Egg Appetizer Dip 36
69. Deviled Eggs I 37
70. Easy Apple Crisp 37
71. Easy Awesome Shrimp Scampi 37
72. Easy Baked Pumpkin Pudding 38
73. Easy Corn Pudding 38
74. Easy Cranberry Orange Relish 39
75. Easy Cranberry Raspberry Sauce 39
76. Easy Crustless Pumpkin Pie 39
77. Easy Garden Green Beans 40
78. Easy Gravy 40
79. Easy Instant Pot® Cranberry Sauce 41
80. Easy Leftover Thanksgiving Turkey Pot Pie 41
81. Easy Orange Cranberry Glaze 42
82. Easy Pleasy Mac N Cheesy US Navy Style 42

83. Easy Pumpkin Cream Trifle 43
84. Easy Pumpkin Pancakes 43
85. Easy Pumpkin Pie Smoothie 44
86. Easy Pumpkin Turnovers 44
87. Easy Sausage Cheese Balls 44
88. Easy Slow Cooker Squash 45
89. Easy Smoked Turkey 45
90. Easy Southern Sweet Potato Casserole 46
91. Easy Stuffing 46
92. Easy Turkey Gravy 47
93. Easy Turkey Tetrazzini 47
94. Excellent And Healthy Cornbread 47
95. Fall Apple Pumpkin Shandy 48
96. Famous No Coffee Pumpkin Latte 48
97. French Stuffing 48
98. Fresh Cranberry Sauce 49
99. Fresh Sweet Cranberry Sauce With A Twist 49
100. Funky Fresh Pumpkin Pie 50
101. Garlic Butter Acorn Squash 50
102. Garlic Mashed Cauliflower 51
103. Ginger Cinnamon Cranberry Sauce 51
104. Give Me Seconds Oyster Dressing 51
105. Glazed Carrots 52
106. Glazed Carrots And Brussels Sprouts 52
107. Gluten Free Sausage Gravy 53
108. Graham Cracker Carmelitas 53
109. Grand Marnier Apples With Ice Cream 54
110. Grandma's Wassail 54
111. Grandpop Joe's Challah Bread Stuffing 54
112. Great Aunt D.J.'s Corn Pudding 55
113. Green Bean Casserole 55
114. Green Bean Casserole With Pumpkin Seed Crumble (Eat Clean For Thanksgiving) 56
115. Green Bean And Potato Casserole 57
116. Grilled Turkey Breast With Fresh Sage Leaves 57
117. Holiday Cranberry Punch 58
118. Holiday Ginger Snap Crust 58
119. Homemade Cranberry Ginger Sauce 58
120. Homemade Turkey Gravy 59
121. Homesteader Cornbread 59
122. Honey Glazed Carrots And Pears 60
123. Hot Mulled Wine 60
124. Incredible Red Smashed Potatoes 61
125. Insanely Easy Cranberry Sauce 61
126. Instant Pot® Thanksgiving Dinner 61

127. Instant Pot® Turkey Breast 62
128. Instant Pot® Warm Vegetarian Farro Salad With Cauliflower, Pistachios And Cranberries ... 63
129. Jan's Cranberry Curd 64
130. Kale With Pine Nuts And Shredded Parmesan 64
131. Leftover Thanksgiving Wedge Pies 64
132. Lemon Pepper Green Beans 65
133. Lemon Glazed Carrots 65
134. Maple Buttercream Frosting 66
135. Maple Cinnamon Ham Glaze 66
136. Maple Ginger Cranberry Sauce 66
137. Maple Glazed Butternut Squash 67
138. Maple Glazed Carrots 67
139. Maple Glazed Turkey Roast 68
140. Maple Dijon Brussels Leaf Salad 68
141. Mashed Sweet Potatoes By Jean Carper 69
142. Mexican Turkey 69
143. Mini Pecan Pie 69
144. Mini Southern Pecan Pies 70
145. Moe's Fabulous Mashed Potatoes 70
146. Mom's Barbeque Style Turkey 71
147. Mom's Candied Yams With Caramel 71
148. Mom's Green Bean Vegetable Casserole ... 72
149. Mother In Law Eggs 72
150. Muffin Tin Potatoes Gratin 73
151. Mushroom Cream Gravy Sauce 73
152. Nanny's Grape Salad 74
153. No Cook Cranberry Salad 74
154. Nutmeg Mashed Potatoes 75
155. Outrageously Good Holiday Salad 75
156. Oven Roasted Turkey Breast 75
157. Parmesan Baskets 76
158. Parmesan Pull Aparts 76
159. Pear Honey Cranberry Sauce 77
160. Pecan Cranberry Butter Tarts 77
161. Pecan Pie Cookies 78
162. Perfect Turkey Gravy 78
163. Pineapple Cranberry Relish 79
164. Pomegranate Cranberry Sauce/Relish 79
165. Potato Pancakes II 80
166. Potato Waffles 80
167. Potato And Parsnip Gratin 80
168. Pretzel Topped Sweet Potatoes 81
169. Pumpkin Bisque (Dairy Free) 82
170. Pumpkin Chipotle Pasta Sauce 82
171. Pumpkin Dump Cake 82

172. Pumpkin Pie Cake II 83
173. Pumpkin Pie Cocktail 83
174. Pumpkin Pie French Toast 84
175. Pumpkin Pie Soup 84
176. Pumpkin Popovers 85
177. Pumpkin Smoothie 85
178. Pumpkin Soup The Easy Way 85
179. Pumpkin Spice Russian 86
180. Quick Brown Rice And Mushroom Pilaf . 86
181. Quick Brussels And Bacon 87
182. Quick Caramel Apple Pie 87
183. Quick Cranberry Butter 87
184. Quick Cranberry Relish 88
185. Quick Gingerbread Latte 88
186. Quick Pumpkin Cake 89
187. Quick Pumpkin Spice Latte 89
188. Quick Turkey And Rice 89
189. Quick Yeast Rolls 90
190. Quick And Easy Pumpkin Mousse 90
191. Quick And Easy Pumpkin Pie Milkshake . 91
192. Quick And Easy Sausage Stuffing 91
193. Quinoa Stuffing 92
194. Really Easy Bread Stuffing 92
195. Red Wine Poached Pears With Chocolate Filling 92
196. Renee's Pumpkin Apple Butter 93
197. Rich Turkey Gravy 93
198. Roasted Brussels Sprouts With Apples, Golden Raisins, And Walnuts 94
199. Roasted Butternut Squash With Onions, Spinach, And Craisins® 94
200. Roasted Peppers With Pine Nuts And Parsley 95
201. Roasted Turkey Criolla Marinade 95
202. Rosemary Sage Squash Seeds 96
203. Sally's Spinach Mashed Potatoes 96
204. Sarah's Frozen Pumpkin Spice Cocktail ... 97
205. Sausage Oyster Dressing 97
206. Scott's Sweet Potato And Butternut Squash Mashers 98
207. Sesame Green Beans 98
208. Simple Deep Fried Turkey 98
209. Simple Mashed Sweet Potato Casserole ... 99
210. Simple Pumpkin Pie 99
211. Simple Roasted Butternut Squash 100
212. Skinny Mashed Potatoes 100
213. Special Turkey Gravy 101

214. Spiced Maple Pumpkin Seeds 101
215. Spiced Turkey Roast 101
216. Spicy Chipotle Sweet Potato Soup 102
217. Spicy Portuguese Stuffing Balls 102
218. Squash Pie 103
219. Squash And Green Bean Saute Side Dish 103
220. Stuffed Delicata Squash 104
221. Stuffed Turkey London Broil 104
222. Summer Squash And Onion Cheesy Casserole 105
223. Sweet Corn Casserole 106
224. Sweet Onion Broccoli Cornbread 106
225. Sweet Potato Cranberry Bake 106
226. Sweet Potato Eggnog Casserole 107
227. Sweet Potato Sage Balls 107
228. Tequila And Orange Cranberry Sauce 108
229. Thanksgiving Any Day Rollups 108
230. Thanksgiving Bacon Stuffing 109
231. Thanksgiving Cookies 109
232. Thanksgiving Quesadilla 109
233. Thanksgiving Spinach Salad 110
234. The Best Banana Pudding 110
235. Thyme Roasted Sweet Potatoes 111
236. Turkey Divan 111
237. Turkey Paupiettes With Apple Maple Stuffing 112
238. Turkey Scallopini And Squash Ravioli With Cranberry Brown Butter 112
239. Turkey Tenderloins 113
240. Turkey A La King 114
241. Two Ingredient Pumpkin Cake 114
242. Vintage Fresh Green Bean Casserole (circa 1956) 114
243. Warm Brie And Pear Tartlets 115
244. Wet Turkey Apple Brine 115
245. White Chocolate Chip Pumpkin Cupcakes 116
246. White Sauce 116
247. White Wine Turkey Gravy 116
248. Yellow Squash Casserole 117
249. Zena's Cranberry Apple Cider Punch 117
250. Zucchilattas 118

INDEX **119**

CONCLUSION **122**

250 Awesome Quick And Easy Thanksgiving Recipes

***

1. After Thanksgiving Casserole

Serving: 6 | Prep: 15mins | Ready in:

Ingredients

- 1/2 cup butter
- 1 cup chopped celery
- 1/4 cup minced onion
- 1 (8 ounce) package bread stuffing cubes
- 1 cup chicken broth
- 2 cups turkey gravy
- 2 cups chopped cooked turkey
- 1 (15 ounce) can cream-style corn
- 3 cups mashed potatoes
- 1/2 cup shredded Cheddar cheese

Direction

- Turn oven to 350°F (175°C) to preheat.
- Heat butter over medium heat in an oven-safe skillet; cook while stirring onion and celery in melted butter for about 10 minutes until onion is tender. Add chicken broth and bread cubes; mix well.
- In a mixing bowl, combine turkey and gravy; spread over stuffing mixture. Place corn over turkey gravy. Top with a layer of mashed potatoes.
- Bake casserole for 20 minutes in the preheated oven until thoroughly heated. Scatter top with Cheddar cheese; place the dish back into the oven. Keep baking for about 10 minutes or until cheese is melted.

Nutrition Information

- Calories: 612 calories;
- Sodium: 1913
- Total Carbohydrate: 67.5
- Cholesterol: 89
- Protein: 25.6
- Total Fat: 26.2

2. Apple Cider Sweet Potatoes

Serving: 4 | Prep: 10mins | Ready in:

Ingredients

- 3 pounds sweet potatoes, peeled and cubed
- 1 cup apple cider
- 1/2 teaspoon salt
- 1 tablespoon butter
- 1 pinch ground black pepper

Direction

- In a big pot, mix together salt, apple cider and sweet potatoes over high heat. Bring to a boil. Lower the heat and simmer, covered, for 20 to 30 minutes until potatoes are softened.
- Mash together cider and potatoes until mixture is smooth. Stir in butter and add pepper to season.

Nutrition Information

- Calories: 352 calories;
- Total Fat: 3.1
- Sodium: 505
- Total Carbohydrate: 76.9
- Cholesterol: 8
- Protein: 5.4

3. Apple Oatmeal Bar Cookies

Serving: 36 | Prep: 15mins | Ready in:

Ingredients

- 1/2 cup butter, softened
- 1 cup packed brown sugar
- 2 1/2 cups uncooked rolled oats
- 1 cup all-purpose flour
- 2 teaspoons ground cinnamon
- 1 teaspoon vanilla extract
- 1/4 cup applesauce
- 1 cup chopped walnuts

Direction

- Set the oven to 175°C or 350°F to preheat. Coat a 13"x9" baking pan slightly with grease.
- Cream brown sugar and butter together in a big bowl until smooth. Beat in vanilla, cinnamon, flour and oats, then fold in walnuts and applesauce. Remove the mixture to the prepped pan.
- In the preheated oven, bake until it turns golden brown, or about 35 minutes. Allow to cool in pan and cut into squares.

Nutrition Information

- Calories: 103 calories;
- Total Fat: 5.1
- Sodium: 20
- Total Carbohydrate: 13.2
- Cholesterol: 7
- Protein: 1.6

4. Apple Pudding

Serving: 6 | Prep: 15mins | Ready in:

Ingredients

- 6 tart apples - peeled, cored and sliced
- 1/4 cup all-purpose flour
- 1 cup sugar
- 1 pinch salt
- 2 cups milk

Direction

- Set an oven to preheat to 165°C (325°F).
- Toss the apples together with salt, sugar and flour and put it in a 9x9-inch baking dish. Put enough milk to the dish to reach nearly the surface of the apples, but don't cover it.
- Let it bake for 45 minutes in the preheated oven, until the apples become tender.

Nutrition Information

- Calories: 260 calories;
- Total Fat: 1.9
- Sodium: 35
- Total Carbohydrate: 60.2
- Cholesterol: 7
- Protein: 3.6

5. Apple Sausage Stuffing

Serving: 8 | Prep: 15mins | Ready in:

Ingredients

- 8 ounces chicken apple sausage links
- 1/2 cup margarine
- 1 large onion, chopped
- 1 cup chopped celery
- 3 apples - peeled, cored, and finely chopped
- 6 ounces corn bread stuffing mix
- 6 ounces seasoned stuffing mix
- 1 1/2 teaspoons poultry seasoning
- 1 pinch salt and ground black pepper to taste
- 1 1/2 cups chicken broth
- 2 eggs, beaten

Direction

- Preheat an oven to 165°C/325°F.
- Cook sausages till heated through and browned for 7-10 minutes in a skillet on medium high heat. Take it off the heat; cut sausages into bite-sized pieces.
- Melt margarine in a big skillet on medium heat. Mix and cook celery and onion in margarine for 7-10 minutes till soft. Put skillet contents in a big bowl.
- Mix apples and sausage into onion mixture. Add black pepper, salt, poultry seasoning, seasoned stuffing mix and cornbread stuffing mix; stir well. Mix eggs and chicken broth into stuffing mixture; put mixture in a 3-qt. baking dish, then use aluminum foil to cover dish.
- In the preheated oven, bake for 20 minutes. Remove aluminum foil from the dish; bake for 10-15 minutes till crisp on top and browned.

Nutrition Information

- Calories: 384 calories;
- Sodium: 1254
- Total Carbohydrate: 41.9
- Cholesterol: 93
- Protein: 12.6
- Total Fat: 18.8

6. Apple Walnut Salad

Serving: 8 | Prep: 20mins | Ready in:

Ingredients

- 3/4 cup brown sugar
- 1 teaspoon ground cinnamon
- 1 (8 ounce) package cream cheese, softened
- 1 (6 ounce) container nonfat plain yogurt
- 1 teaspoon vanilla
- 6 large apples - peeled, cored and chopped
- 1 1/2 cups chopped walnuts
- 1 cup dried cranberries
- 1/4 cup chopped walnuts

Direction

- In a large bowl, combine cinnamon and brown sugar. Whisk in vanilla, yogurt and softened cream cheese until mixture becomes smooth.
- Stir dried cranberries, apples and 1 1/2 cups of walnuts into the cream cheese mixture, stir until well coated.
- Place salad in a serving bowl using a spoon and decorate with remaining 1/4 cup of chopped walnuts. Refrigerate until serving.

Nutrition Information

- Calories: 459 calories;
- Total Fat: 26.8
- Sodium: 105
- Total Carbohydrate: 53.9
- Cholesterol: 31
- Protein: 7.7

7. Apple And Pumpkin Dessert

Serving: 1 | Prep: 5mins | Ready in:

Ingredients

- 2 (1 gram) packets sugar substitute
- 1 teaspoon pumpkin pie spice
- 1 Granny Smith apple - peeled, cored and chopped
- 1/4 cup canned pumpkin
- 2 tablespoons water

Direction

- In a microwave-safe bowl, sprinkle 1/3 teaspoon pumpkin pie spice and 1/3 packet of sugar substitute. Layer a quarter of the apple slices into the bowl; repeat to make another layer. Spread pumpkin over the apples. Take the remaining pumpkin pie spice and sugar substitute and sprinkle them on the pumpkin.

Top with the rest of the apples. Pour water onto mixture.
- Place bowl inside the microwave and cook for 3 1/2 minute on high power, stirring after each minute.

Nutrition Information

- Calories: 88 calories;
- Sodium: 151
- Total Carbohydrate: 23.8
- Cholesterol: 0
- Protein: 1.2
- Total Fat: 0.4

8. Asparagus With Cranberries And Pine Nuts

Serving: 4 | Prep: 10mins | Ready in:

Ingredients

- 1 bunch asparagus
- 3 tablespoons olive oil
- 1/3 cup pine nuts
- 1/3 cup dried cranberries
- 1 pinch salt

Direction

- Trim or break off the woody ends from asparagus and throw them away. Put the spears aside.
- In a skillet, heat olive oil on moderate heat. Stir in salt, cranberries, pine nuts, then cook and stir for 5-6 minutes, until pine nuts begin to look translucent. Put in asparagus spears and cook for 5-8 minutes while putting in a small amount of olive oil if necessary, until stalks are soft and bright green. To serve, put asparagus on a platter and scoop nuts and cranberries on top.

Nutrition Information

- Calories: 206 calories;
- Cholesterol: 0
- Protein: 5.2
- Total Fat: 16
- Sodium: 3
- Total Carbohydrate: 14.3

9. Australian Style Pumpkin Scones

Serving: 12 | Prep: 15mins | Ready in:

Ingredients

- 1 tablespoon butter, at room temperature
- 2 cups self-rising flour
- 1/2 cup white sugar
- 1 teaspoon baking powder
- 1/4 teaspoon salt
- 1 cup cooked and mashed pumpkin
- 1 egg

Direction

- Preheat the oven to 230 degrees C (450 degrees F).
- Use your fingers to brush the butter into flour in a bowl until combined evenly. Add salt, baking powder, and sugar into the flour mixture and form a well in the center. In a separate bowl, combine egg and pumpkin and then add to the well. Stir until dough is mixed well. Onto a floured work surface, flip the dough and use a knife coated with flour to cut it into squares. Spread the squares in a baking sheet.
- Bake for about 15 to 20 minutes in the preheated oven until browned lightly.

Nutrition Information

- Calories: 128 calories;

- Total Fat: 1.6
- Sodium: 416
- Total Carbohydrate: 25.6
- Cholesterol: 18
- Protein: 2.8

10. Autumn Apple Salad II

Serving: 4 | Prep: 10mins | Ready in:

Ingredients

- 4 tart green apples, cored and chopped
- 1/4 cup blanched slivered almonds, toasted
- 1/4 cup dried cranberries
- 1/4 cup chopped dried cherries
- 1 (8 ounce) container vanilla yogurt

Direction

- In a medium-size bowl, mix together yogurt, cherries, cranberries, almonds, and apples until coated evenly.

Nutrition Information

- Calories: 202 calories;
- Protein: 5.1
- Total Fat: 4.1
- Sodium: 41
- Total Carbohydrate: 38.9
- Cholesterol: 3

11. Autumn Stuffed Acorn Squash

Serving: 4 | Prep: 15mins | Ready in:

Ingredients

- 2 acorn squash, halved and seeded
- 1 1/2 teaspoons dark brown sugar
- 1/4 teaspoon ground cinnamon
- salt and ground black pepper to taste
- 1 tablespoon butter, cut in small pieces
- 1 (16 ounce) package maple-flavored breakfast sausage
- 1 cup cooked wild rice
- 1/2 cup dried cranberries
- 1/4 cup chicken stock

Direction

- Preheat an oven to 175°C/350°F.
- Put squash halves in roasting pan, cut side up; run fork through meat of every half making grooves. Sprinkle pepper, salt, cinnamon and brown sugar; use butter pieces to dot.
- In preheated oven, bake for 30-40 minutes till meat is tender so a fork can puncture it.
- Heat big skillet on medium high heat; mix and cook sausage in hot skillet for 5-7 minutes till crumbly and browned. Drain; discard grease. Add chicken stock, cranberries and wild rice; mix and cook for 5 minutes till cranberries and rice absorb chicken stock.
- In each squash half, put sausage filling. Put stuffed squash in oven; bake for 5-10 minutes till flavors are blended.

Nutrition Information

- Calories: 506 calories;
- Total Fat: 27.7
- Sodium: 1085
- Total Carbohydrate: 49.3
- Cholesterol: 73
- Protein: 19.1

12. Bacon Wrapped Pork Medallions

Serving: 4 | Prep: 10mins | Ready in:

Ingredients

- 8 slices bacon

- 1 tablespoon garlic powder
- 1 teaspoon seasoned salt
- 1 teaspoon dried basil
- 1 teaspoon dried oregano
- 2 pounds pork tenderloin
- 2 tablespoons butter
- 2 tablespoons olive oil

Direction

- Turn the oven to 400°F (200°C) to preheat.
- In a big, oven-safe frying pan, cook bacon over medium-high heat for 6-7 minutes until remaining flexible and turning light brown, flipping sometimes. Put the bacon slices on a dish lined with paper towels to strain. Discard the excess bacon fat from the frying pan. In a small bowl, mix together oregano, basil, seasoning salt, and garlic powder. Put aside.
- Wrap bacon strips around the pork tenderloin and use 1-2 toothpicks to keep each bacon strip in place. Between each bacon strip, cut the tenderloin to form the medallions. Coat both sides of the medallions with the seasoning mix by dipping. In the same frying pan, heat oil and butter over medium-high heat to melt. Cook each side of the medallion for 4 minutes.
- Put the frying pan in the preheated oven and bake for 17-20 minutes until the middle of the pork is not pink anymore. An instant-read thermometer should display 145°F (63°C) when you insert it into the middle.

Nutrition Information

- Calories: 417 calories;
- Total Carbohydrate: 2.4
- Cholesterol: 133
- Protein: 42.3
- Total Fat: 25.5
- Sodium: 769

13. Bacon Wrapped Turkey Breast Stuffed With Spinach And Feta

Serving: 4 | Prep: 15mins | Ready in:

Ingredients

- 1 large turkey breast
- 1/2 teaspoon dried oregano
- 1/2 teaspoon ground cumin
- salt and ground black pepper to taste
- 1 cup fresh spinach, or to taste
- 1/4 cup crumbled feta cheese
- 12 slices reduced-sodium bacon, or as needed

Direction

- Prepare the oven and set to 350°F or 175°C.
- Make a slice in the middle of the turkey breast and place it flat. Drizzle salt, cumin, oregano and pepper on the side of the turkey. Place a layer of spinach leaves on one of the turkey and top with feta cheese. Repeat the process of layering with feta cheese and spinach. Then, fold the other turkey breast half over the feta cheese to seal the filling. Take the bacon and wrap the whole turkey breast with it. Put the wrapped turkey in a baking dish and dash with salt and pepper.
- Let the turkey breast cook for about half an hour or until an instant read thermometer inserted into the center reads at least 165°F /74 degrees C or until no longer pink in the center and juices run clear.
- Turn the oven's broiler on and broil the wrapped turkey for 2 minutes per side until the bacon becomes crisp on each side. Let it cool for about ten minutes before cutting.

Nutrition Information

- Calories: 371 calories;
- Total Fat: 27.6
- Sodium: 688
- Total Carbohydrate: 1.4
- Cholesterol: 82
- Protein: 27.7

14. Bacon And Almond Green Bean Casserole

Serving: 10 | Prep: 10mins | Ready in:

Ingredients

- 6 slices thick-cut bacon
- 1 1/2 cups whole milk
- 2 (10.75 ounce) cans condensed cream of mushroom soup
- 1/2 cup sliced almonds
- 3/4 teaspoon garlic-pepper seasoning
- 3/4 (6 ounce) can French-fried onions
- 4 (14.5 ounce) cans green beans (such as Del Monte® Fresh Cut®), drained
- 1/4 (6 ounce) can French-fried onions

Direction

- Start preheating the oven to 350°F (175°C).
- In a big frying pan, cook bacon over medium-high heat for 10 minutes until turning evenly brown, flipping sometimes. Put on paper towels to strain, crumble into pieces, about 1 inch each.
- In a big bowl, combine cream of mushroom soup and milk together. Add 3/4 can French-fried onion, garlic pepper, and almonds; toss to blend. Gently nestle green beans into the mixture. Add to a 9x9-in. glass or ceramic baking dish.
- Put in the preheated oven and bake for 20 minutes until bubbling and fully cooked. Put the leftover 1/4 can French-fried onions on top; bake for 3-4 minutes until the onions turn light brown.

Nutrition Information

- Calories: 277 calories;
- Sodium: 1139
- Total Carbohydrate: 21.1
- Cholesterol: 10
- Protein: 7.1
- Total Fat: 18.1

15. Bacon Garlic Green Beans

Serving: 12 | Prep: 15mins | Ready in:

Ingredients

- 3 pounds fresh green beans, trimmed
- 4 slices bacon
- 1 cup butter
- 4 cloves garlic, minced
- 1/2 teaspoon lemon zest

Direction

- Boil a pot of green beans covered with water. Lower the heat to medium low and simmer for 10 minutes until beans start softening. Remove the water, and leave the beans in pot.
- On a microwavable plate, place the bacon strips and microwave it for 2 minutes until crispy. Let bacon cool then crumble.
- Add bacon and butter to the pot of beans. Set the heat to medium, and cook for 2-3 minutes to melt the butter. Add some garlic, stirring it for 34 minutes until aromatic. Add lemon zest on top and stir.

Nutrition Information

- Calories: 189 calories;
- Cholesterol: 44
- Protein: 3.4
- Total Fat: 16.7
- Sodium: 185
- Total Carbohydrate: 8.5

16. Baked Acorn Squash With Apple Stuffing

Serving: 2 | Prep: 15mins | Ready in:

Ingredients

- 1 tablespoon olive oil
- 1 acorn squash, halved and seeded
- 1 apple, diced
- 2 tablespoons diced celery
- 2 tablespoons water
- 2 teaspoons minced onion
- 2 teaspoons butter, cubed
- 1 teaspoon maple syrup
- 1 pinch ground cinnamon, or to taste

Direction

- Preheat an oven to 200°C/400°F; grease baking sheet using olive oil lightly.
- Put squash on baking sheet, cut side down.
- Mix butter, onion, water, celery and apple in small baking dish; use aluminum foil to cover.
- In preheated oven, bake apple mixture and squash for 45 minutes till apple and squash are tender. Use apple mixture to fill squash halves; drizzle maple syrup then sprinkle cinnamon.

Nutrition Information

- Calories: 244 calories;
- Sodium: 44
- Total Carbohydrate: 38.8
- Cholesterol: 11
- Protein: 2.3
- Total Fat: 11.2

17. Baked Corn Casserole

Serving: 8 | Prep: 10mins | Ready in:

Ingredients

- 1 teaspoon vegetable oil
- 1/2 cup chopped onion
- 1/4 cup butter, softened
- 2 (3 ounce) packages cream cheese, softened
- 1 (15.25 ounce) can whole kernel corn, drained
- 1 (15.25 ounce) can creamed corn
- 1 (4 ounce) can chopped green chile peppers
- 1 (2.8 ounce) package French-fried onions, divided

Direction

- Set oven to 350°F (175°C) to preheat. Oil an 8-by 8-inch baking dish.
- In a small skillet, heat oil over medium heat. Sauté onion till transparent.
- Combine cream cheese and butter in a large mixing bowl. Mix in onions, chile peppers, creamed corn, and whole kernel corn. Transfer mixture to the prepared baking dish.
- Bake for 15 minutes in the preheated oven. Take the dish out of the oven and mix in 1/2 of the fried onions; scatter remaining onions over the top. Bake for another 15 minutes.

Nutrition Information

- Calories: 282 calories;
- Sodium: 666
- Total Carbohydrate: 26.2
- Cholesterol: 39
- Protein: 4.3
- Total Fat: 19.4

18. Balsamic Butternut Squash With Kale

Serving: 6 | Prep: 15mins | Ready in:

Ingredients

- 12 ounces butternut squash - peeled, seeded, and cut into 1-inch pieces
- 1 small yellow onion, cut into 1/2-inch pieces

- 3 tablespoons balsamic vinegar, divided
- 1 tablespoon brown sugar
- 2 teaspoons vegetable oil
- kosher salt and ground black pepper to taste
- 6 ounces kale, roughly chopped
- 1/4 cup vegetable broth

Direction

- Preheat an oven to 200°C/400°F.
- Toss pepper, salt, vegetable oil, brown sugar, 1/2 balsamic vinegar, onion and squash to coat in a bowl; spread it onto baking sheet in 1 layer.
- In preheated oven, bake for 30-40 minutes till squash is golden and tender.
- Lightly simmer broth and kale in a heavy-bottom skillet. Cover skillet; lower heat. Cook for 5 minutes till kale is tender yet bright green; drain extra liquid. Mix leftover balsamic vinegar, squash mixture and kale in a serving bowl.

Nutrition Information

- Calories: 72 calories;
- Total Fat: 1.8
- Sodium: 103
- Total Carbohydrate: 14.1
- Cholesterol: 0
- Protein: 1.7

19. Banana Pudding IV

Serving: 12 | Prep: 30mins | Ready in:

Ingredients

- 1 (8 ounce) package cream cheese
- 1 (14 ounce) can sweetened condensed milk
- 1 (5 ounce) package instant vanilla pudding mix
- 3 cups cold milk
- 1 teaspoon vanilla extract
- 1 (8 ounce) container frozen whipped topping, thawed
- 4 bananas, sliced
- 1/2 (12 ounce) package vanilla wafers

Direction

- Beat cream cheese in a large bowl until fluffy. Beat in vanilla, cold milk, pudding mix and condensed milk until smooth. Add half of the whipped topping by folding in.
- Use vanilla wafers to line the bottom of a 9x13 inch dish. Lay sliced bananas over the wafers evenly. Add pudding mixture on top and spread out. Use the remaining whipped topping to top. Let it chill.

Nutrition Information

- Calories: 398 calories;
- Total Fat: 16.6
- Sodium: 333
- Total Carbohydrate: 55.1
- Cholesterol: 37
- Protein: 7

20. Basic Corn Muffins

Serving: 12 | Prep: 10mins | Ready in:

Ingredients

- 1 cup cornmeal
- 1 cup all-purpose flour
- 1/3 cup white sugar
- 2 teaspoons baking powder
- 1/2 teaspoon salt
- 1 egg, beaten
- 1/4 cup canola oil
- 1 cup milk

Direction

- Preheat the oven to 200°C or 400°F. Line using paper muffin liners or oil muffin pan.

- Combine together salt, baking powder, sugar, flour and corn meal in a big bowl. Put milk, oil and egg; slowly mix to incorporate. Spoon batter into the prepped muffin cups.
- Bake for 15 to 20 minutes at 200°C or 400°F or till a toothpick pricked into a muffin comes out clean.

Nutrition Information

- Calories: 154 calories;
- Sodium: 196
- Total Carbohydrate: 22.5
- Cholesterol: 17
- Protein: 3.1
- Total Fat: 5.9

21. Basic Mashed Potatoes

Serving: 4 | Prep: 15mins | Ready in:

Ingredients

- 2 pounds baking potatoes, peeled and quartered
- 2 tablespoons butter
- 1 cup milk
- salt and pepper to taste

Direction

- Boil the pot of salted water. Put in the potatoes and cook for roughly 15 minutes till soft yet still firm; drain off.
- In the small-sized saucepan, heat the milk and butter on low heat till the butter melts. With the electric beater or potato masher, gradually blend the milk mixture into the potatoes till creamy and smooth. Use the pepper and salt to season to taste.

Nutrition Information

- Calories: 257 calories;
- Total Carbohydrate: 43.7
- Cholesterol: 20
- Protein: 5.6
- Total Fat: 7.2
- Sodium: 76

22. Basic Yankee Bread Stuffing

Serving: 12 | Prep: 10mins | Ready in:

Ingredients

- 1 pound ground pork sausage
- 1 tablespoon butter
- 6 stalks chopped celery
- 2 onions, chopped
- 2 (1 pound) loaves day-old white bread, torn into small pieces
- 1 1/2 teaspoons sage seasoning mixture
- salt and pepper to taste
- 2 eggs, lightly beaten
- 1 cup chicken broth

Direction

- Prepare the oven by preheating to 325°F (165°C). Prepare a 9x13-inch baking dish that is lightly greased.
- In a big, deep skillet, put in the pork sausage. Then cook on medium-high heat until equally brown. Strain and reserve.
- In a big saucepan set on medium heat, dissolve butter. Add onion and celery in the saucepan, then gradually stir and cook until it is tender.
- In a big bowl, combine pepper, salt, sage, bread, onions, celery, and sausage.
- Add the chicken and the eggs in the mixture. Add more broth if necessary. The stuffing should be damp, not mushy.
- Then press mixture in the baking dish. Place in the preheated oven and bake for 1 hour, or until crisp and brown on top.

Nutrition Information

- Calories: 329 calories;
- Sodium: 888
- Total Carbohydrate: 41
- Cholesterol: 55
- Protein: 12.3
- Total Fat: 12.5

23. Bernie's Big Batch "Apple Pie In A Jar" Jam

Serving: 224 | Prep: 30mins | Ready in:

Ingredients

- 12 cups smooth applesauce
- 8 cups peeled and chopped apples
- 8 1/2 cups white sugar
- 6 cups firmly packed brown sugar
- 2 teaspoons ground cinnamon
- 1 teaspoon ground nutmeg
- 1/4 cup butter
- 2 (3 ounce) pouches liquid pectin (such as CERTO®)
- 28 half-pint canning jars with lids and rings

Direction

- Put nutmeg, cinnamon, brown sugar, white sugar, apples and applesauce in a big pot; add butter. Mix and cook on medium high heat for 1 minute till it boils. Mix in liquid pectin quickly; boil for 1 minute longer. Take off heat.
- Sterilize lids and jars for a minimum of 5 minutes in boiling water. Pack ham in sterilized hot jars; fill each to within 1/4-in. of top. Run a thin spatula/clean knife around inside of the jars to remove air bubbles after filling them. Use a moist paper towel to wipe jars' rims to remove any food residue. Put lids over; screw on rings.
- Put a rack on bottom of a big stockpot, then use water to fill halfway. Boil; use a holder to lower jars in boiling water, 2-in. between jars.

If needed, add extra boiling water so water level is at least 1-in. above jars' tops. Put water on a rolling boil and cover pot; process jars for 10 minutes.
- Take jars from the stockpot, then put on a wood/cloth-covered surface till cool, a few inches apart till cool. Use a finger to press top of each lid; make sure the seal is tight and lid doesn't move down or up at all. Keep in a dark, cool area.

Nutrition Information

- Calories: 62 calories;
- Total Fat: 0.2
- Sodium: 3
- Total Carbohydrate: 15.5
- Cholesterol: 1
- Protein: 0

24. Best Ever Pecan Pie Bars

Serving: 24 | Prep: 20mins | Ready in:

Ingredients

- 2 cups all-purpose flour
- 1/2 cup confectioners' sugar
- 1 cup butter, softened
- 1 (14 ounce) can sweetened condensed milk
- 1 (8 ounce) package toffee baking bits (such as Heath®)
- 1 cup chopped pecans
- 1 egg

Direction

- Start preheating the oven to 350°F (175°C).
- Combine butter, confectioners' sugar, and flour in a bowl; press into a 9x13-inch baking pan.
- Bake in the prepared oven for about 15 minutes until lightly browned.

- Stir egg, pecans, toffee baking bits, and sweetened condensed milk together in a bowl; spread over the hot crust.
- Bake for additional 25 minutes in the prepared oven until bubbling and browned. Let cool before serving.

Nutrition Information

- Calories: 211 calories;
- Total Fat: 13.2
- Sodium: 86
- Total Carbohydrate: 20.9
- Cholesterol: 35
- Protein: 3.1

25. Black Friday Sandwich

Serving: 1 | Prep: 10mins | Ready in:

Ingredients

- 1 tablespoon canned jellied cranberry sauce
- 1 tablespoon mayonnaise
- 1/4 teaspoon celery seed
- 2 slices bread
- 1 tablespoon mashed leftover sweet potato casserole with marshmallow topping
- 1 tablespoon gravy (optional)
- 1 tablespoon dry leftover stuffing
- 1/4 cup shredded leftover cooked turkey
- 1 tablespoon coarsely chopped leftover green bean casserole
- 1 tablespoon chopped French-fried onions

Direction

- In a bowl, use a fork to mash cranberry sauce until it becomes smooth. Put in celery seed and mayonnaise; blend through. Spread sauce on top of bread slices.
- Spread over 1 slice of bread with sweet potato casserole.
- In a bowl, mash together stuffing and gravy. Put in turkey and mix. Scoop the mixture on top of the sweet potatoes; put onions and green bean casserole over. Top with second slice of bread.

Nutrition Information

- Calories: 489 calories;
- Total Fat: 25.5
- Sodium: 804
- Total Carbohydrate: 47.8
- Cholesterol: 34
- Protein: 15.6

26. Black Friday Turkey Salad

Serving: 8 | Prep: 20mins | Ready in:

Ingredients

- 1/2 cup mayonnaise (such as Hellman's®)
- 3 tablespoons prepared yellow mustard (such as Plochman's®)
- 2 tablespoons crumbled cooked bacon
- 3/4 cup shredded Cheddar cheese
- 2 tablespoons dill pickle relish
- 1/2 cup finely chopped pepperoncini
- 1/8 teaspoon crushed red pepper
- salt, to taste
- 2 cups coarsely chopped leftover turkey

Direction

- In a big bowl, mix salt, mayonnaise, red pepper, mustard, pepperoncini, bacon, relish, and Cheddar cheese; mix in turkey to coat.

Nutrition Information

- Calories: 215 calories;
- Sodium: 617
- Total Carbohydrate: 1.5
- Cholesterol: 44

- Protein: 14.2
- Total Fat: 16.9

27. Blackberry Cobbler II

Serving: 8 | Prep: 20mins | Ready in:

Ingredients

- 1 cup all-purpose flour
- 1 1/2 cups white sugar, divided
- 1 teaspoon baking powder
- 1/2 teaspoon salt
- 6 tablespoons cold butter
- 1/4 cup boiling water
- 2 tablespoons cornstarch
- 1/4 cup cold water
- 1 tablespoon lemon juice
- 4 cups fresh blackberries, rinsed and drained

Direction

- Set oven to 400°F (200°C) to preheat. Line a baking tray using aluminum foil.
- Combine the salt, baking powder, 1/2 cup sugar and flour in a big bowl. Stir in butter until the mixture forms coarse crumbs. Mix in 1/4 cup boiling water just until evenly moistened.
- Mix the cornstarch with cold water in another bowl. Stir in blackberries, lemon juice, and leftover 1 cup sugar. Add to a cast iron skillet and heat up to a boil, mixing constantly. Put dough by spoonfuls into the skillet. Put skillet on the baking tray lined with foil.
- Bake in the preheated oven for 25 minutes until golden brown.

Nutrition Information

- Calories: 318 calories;
- Total Carbohydrate: 58.4
- Cholesterol: 23
- Protein: 2.7

- Total Fat: 9.1
- Sodium: 253

28. Blue Cheese And Pear Tartlets

Serving: 15 | Prep: 10mins | Ready in:

Ingredients

- 4 ounces blue cheese, crumbled
- 1 ripe pear - peeled, cored, and chopped
- 2 tablespoons light cream
- ground black pepper to taste
- 1 (2.1 ounce) package mini phyllo tart shells

Direction

- Prepare the phyllo shells following the package instructions; set aside and cool.
- Combine cream, pear, and blue cheese; sprinkle pepper to taste. Scoop the mixture into the cooled phyllo shells.
- Bake in a 175°C or 350°F oven for 15 minutes. Serve hot.

Nutrition Information

- Calories: 60 calories;
- Total Fat: 3.6
- Sodium: 116
- Total Carbohydrate: 4.5
- Cholesterol: 7
- Protein: 2.2

29. Bourbon Glazed Carrots

Serving: 8 | Prep: 10mins | Ready in:

Ingredients

- 2 pounds carrots, peeled and sliced diagonally into 1/2-inch pieces

- 1/4 cup brown sugar
- 1/4 cup butter, melted
- 2 tablespoons bourbon, or more to taste

Direction

- In a big pot, add carrots and water to cover, then bring to a boil. Lower heat to moderately low and simmer for 10-15 minutes, until softened yet still firm to the bite. Drain and turn to a serving bowl.
- In a saucepan, mix together bourbon, butter and brown sugar, then bring the mixture to a simmer. Cook and stir for 10 minutes, until it is thickened. Drizzle over carrots with sauce and serve promptly.

Nutrition Information

- Calories: 132 calories;
- Total Carbohydrate: 17.6
- Cholesterol: 15
- Protein: 1.1
- Total Fat: 6
- Sodium: 121

30. Brie Cheese Pizza

Serving: 16 | Prep: 10mins | Ready in:

Ingredients

- 8 1/2 ounces Brie cheese, thinly sliced
- 2 cups sliced almonds
- 1 (14 ounce) package purchased fully baked pizza crust (such as Boboli®)

Direction

- Start preheating the oven to 350°F (175°C).
- On a pizza crust, put slices of Brie, put on sliced almonds to cover. Bake for 10 minutes until the almonds have toasted and the cheese has melted. Cut into small wedges and serve.

Nutrition Information

- Calories: 228 calories;
- Total Fat: 14.7
- Sodium: 240
- Total Carbohydrate: 16.1
- Cholesterol: 18
- Protein: 10.4

31. Brie, Cranberries, And Pistachio Wreath

Serving: 6 | Prep: 15mins | Ready in:

Ingredients

- 1 (8 ounce) round puff pastry sheet
- 3 tablespoons cranberry sauce
- 6 ounces Brie cheese, sliced
- 2 tablespoons chopped pistachio nuts
- 1 egg, beaten
- 1 teaspoon dried rosemary

Direction

- Preheat the oven to 200 ° C or 400 ° F. Line parchment paper on a baking sheet.
- On prepped baking sheet, spread puff pastry. Put one 4-inches bowl upside facing down in the middle; using paring knife, mark a round and from the middle to edge of marked round, create 4 cuts, creating a shape like star. Take bowl off. Scatter cranberry sauce on dough center surrounding; put pistachios and Brie slices on top.
- Put pastry outer edge and a point of star inwards on top of filling; pinch together. Redo with the other dough pieces, till it looks much like a wreath. Brush with the beaten egg and scatter rosemary over.
- In the prepped oven, bake for 15 minutes, till golden brown and Brie cheese has melted partially. Take out of oven and rest for 5 minutes prior to serving.

Nutrition Information

- Calories: 341 calories;
- Total Fat: 24.2
- Sodium: 296
- Total Carbohydrate: 21.3
- Cholesterol: 56
- Protein: 10.1

32. Broccoli Cheese Squares

Serving: 6 | Prep: 15mins | Ready in:

Ingredients

- 1/4 cup butter
- 2 (10 ounce) packages frozen broccoli florets, thawed and drained
- 1 pound shredded sharp Cheddar cheese
- 1 cup milk
- 1 cup all-purpose flour
- 3 eggs
- 1 teaspoon baking powder
- 1 teaspoon salt
- ground black pepper to taste

Direction

- Preheat the oven to 175 ° C or 350 ° F. Put the butter in one casserole dish, 9x13-inch in size; in preheating oven, put casserole dish till butter liquifies.
- In a big bowl, combine black pepper, salt, baking powder, eggs, flour, milk, Cheddar cheese and broccoli. In casserole dish, place the mixture on top of liquified butter.
- In prepped oven, bake for 30 to 45 minutes, till casserole turn golden brown on surface and cheese melts. Slice into squares and serve. For best flavor, consume at room temperature.

Nutrition Information

- Calories: 530 calories;
- Total Fat: 36.5

- Sodium: 1068
- Total Carbohydrate: 23.8
- Cholesterol: 196
- Protein: 28.2

33. Brown Sugar N' Bacon Green Beans

Serving: 6 | Prep: 10mins | Ready in:

Ingredients

- 6 slices bacon, or more to taste
- 1/2 cup water
- 1/4 cup brown sugar, or more to taste
- 1 teaspoon vegetable seasoning salt (such as McCormick® Vegetable Supreme® Seasoning)
- 2 pounds fresh green beans, trimmed and halved
- salt to taste

Direction

- In a big skillet, add bacon and cook on moderately high heat for 10 minutes while turning from time to time, until crispy. Remove bacon slices onto paper towels to drain and save 1 tablespoon of bacon drippings, then crumble the bacon.
- In a skillet, bring water to a boil. Put bacon drippings, vegetable seasoning and brown sugar into water, then cook and stir for 2 minutes, until brown sugar dissolves. Put into the brown sugar mixture with bacon and green beans, then use salt to season the mixture. Lower heat and simmer for 10 minutes, until green beans obtain desired tenderness.

Nutrition Information

- Calories: 121 calories;
- Total Fat: 4
- Sodium: 289

- Total Carbohydrate: 17.2
- Cholesterol: 10
- Protein: 6.5

34. Brussels Sprout Slaw

Serving: 6 | Prep: 20mins | Ready in:

Ingredients

- Dressing:
- 1/4 cup olive oil
- 2 tablespoons distilled white vinegar
- 1 tablespoon honey
- 1 clove garlic, minced
- 1 teaspoon brown mustard
- Salad:
- 1 pound Brussels sprouts, shredded
- 1/2 cup dried cherries
- 1/2 cup slivered almonds
- 1/2 cup grated Parmesan cheese

Direction

- In a bowl, mix mustard, olive oil, garlic, vinegar, and honey together until smooth.
- In a bowl, toss Parmesan cheese, Brussels sprouts, almonds, and dried cherries; mix in dressing, toss till coated. Chill for a few hours in the refrigerator to bring out the flavors. Serve.

Nutrition Information

- Calories: 248 calories;
- Total Fat: 15.8
- Sodium: 135
- Total Carbohydrate: 20.6
- Cholesterol: 6
- Protein: 7.8

35. Brussels Sprouts Gratin

Serving: 4 | Prep: 15mins | Ready in:

Ingredients

- 1 pound Brussels sprouts, cleaned and trimmed
- 2 slices bacon, cut into 1/2 inch pieces
- salt and ground black pepper to taste
- 1/2 cup heavy cream
- 1/4 cup bread crumbs
- 1/4 cup grated Parmesan cheese
- 2 tablespoons butter, cut into tiny pieces

Direction

- Preheat the oven to 400°F (200°C). Grease the baking dish lightly.
- Add water and a few pinches of salt into a big pot then lead it to boiling point. Insert Brussels sprouts, cooking for around 8 minutes without any cover on until they tenderize. Use a colander to strain before immersing them in icy water for a few minutes until they become cold enough to put a halt to the cooking activity. The second that the sprouts turn cold start draining them thoroughly then cutting them up into quarters or halves according to the original sizes. Put them to one side. Insert bacon into a big, hollow skillet, cooking them for around 5 minutes at medium high heat until they become a little brown and wilted. Lower the heat before adding the Brussels sprouts, stirring. Add pepper and salt to season before tossing together until evenly distributed with seasoning, around 1 minute. On the prepped baking dish, distribute the Brussels sprouts and bacon followed by pouring in the cream levelly. Over the cream, scatter Parmesan cheese and breadcrumbs then a few bits of butter on top. Put it into the preheated oven. Leave it baking for 20 to 25 minutes until thoroughly heated and browned.

Nutrition Information

- Calories: 312 calories;
- Sodium: 586
- Total Carbohydrate: 15.8
- Cholesterol: 70
- Protein: 8
- Total Fat: 25.4

36. Bulgur Wheat With Dried Cranberries

Serving: 2 | Prep: 10mins | Ready in:

Ingredients

- 1 cup water
- 1/2 cup dry bulgur wheat
- 1 1/2 tablespoons chicken bouillon granules
- 1 teaspoon butter
- 1/4 cup dried cranberries

Direction

- Boil a pot of water, and stir in butter, bouillon granules, and bulgur. Put a cover on the pot, lower the heat to low, and simmer for 15 minutes.
- Using a fork, fluff the cooked bulgur, and lightly stir in the dried cranberries.

Nutrition Information

- Calories: 137 calories;
- Sodium: 865
- Total Carbohydrate: 26.3
- Cholesterol: 6
- Protein: 2.9
- Total Fat: 2.8

37. Butternut Squash Soup II

Serving: 4 | Prep: 25mins | Ready in:

Ingredients

- 2 tablespoons butter
- 1 small onion, chopped
- 1 stalk celery, chopped
- 1 medium carrot, chopped
- 2 medium potatoes, cubed
- 1 medium butternut squash - peeled, seeded, and cubed
- 1 (32 fluid ounce) container chicken stock
- salt and freshly ground black pepper to taste

Direction

- Melt butter in a big pot; cook squash, potatoes, celery, carrot and onion till lightly browned for 5 minutes. Add enough chicken stock in to cover the veggies; boil. Lower the heat to low then cover the pot; simmer till all veggies are tender or for 40 minutes.
- Put the soup into a blender; blend till smooth. Put back into the pot; mix any leftover stock in to get the preferred consistency. Season with pepper and salt.

Nutrition Information

- Calories: 305 calories;
- Sodium: 1151
- Total Carbohydrate: 59.7
- Cholesterol: 21
- Protein: 6.9
- Total Fat: 6.8

38. Butternut Squash And Pecan Casserole

Serving: 8 | Prep: 15mins | Ready in:

Ingredients

- 2 cups mashed, cooked butternut squash
- 1/2 cup chopped onion
- 1/2 cup mayonnaise

- 1/2 cup shredded Cheddar cheese
- 1/4 cup white sugar
- 1 egg
- 1/2 cup cracker crumbs
- 1/4 cup chopped pecans
- 1/4 cup sunflower seeds
- 1/4 cup butter, melted

Direction

- Start preheating the oven at 350°F (175°C).
- Combine egg, sugar, Cheddar cheese, mayonnaise, onion, and butternut squash in a casserole dish.
- Blend sunflower seeds, pecans, and cracker crumbs in a bowl; spread over squash mixture. Transfer melted butter over crumb topping.
- Bake in the prepared oven until bubbling and crumb topping turns brown, 45 minutes.

Nutrition Information

- Calories: 313 calories;
- Total Fat: 24.6
- Sodium: 176
- Total Carbohydrate: 20.3
- Cholesterol: 51
- Protein: 5.2

39. Buttery Garlic Green Beans

Serving: 4 | Prep: 10mins | Ready in:

Ingredients

- 1 pound fresh green beans, trimmed and snapped in half
- 3 tablespoons butter
- 3 cloves garlic, minced
- 2 pinches lemon pepper
- salt to taste

Direction

- In a big skillet, add green beans and water to cover, then bring water to a boil. Lower heat to moderately low and simmer for 5 minutes, until beans begin to soften. Drain water, then put into green beans with butter. Cook and stir for 2-3 minutes, until butter has melted.
- Add garlic, cook and stir together with green beans for 3-4 minutes, until garlic is aromatic and soft. Use salt and lemon pepper to season.

Nutrition Information

- Calories: 116 calories;
- Sodium: 222
- Total Carbohydrate: 8.9
- Cholesterol: 23
- Protein: 2.3
- Total Fat: 8.8

40. Candied Apples II

Serving: 15 | Prep: 10mins | Ready in:

Ingredients

- 15 apples
- 2 cups white sugar
- 1 cup light corn syrup
- 1 1/2 cups water
- 8 drops red food coloring

Direction

- Grease cookie sheets lightly. Into stemmed, whole apples, insert the craft sticks.
- In a medium saucepan, combine water, corn syrup and sugar over medium-high heat. Heat up to between 149 and 154°C (300 and 310°F), or until a little syrup forms hard, brittle threads when being dropped into cold water. Take off heat and mix in the food coloring.
- Hold the apple's stick, dip it in syrup and take out and rotate to evenly coat. Let harden on the prepared cookie sheets.

Nutrition Information

- Calories: 237 calories;
- Cholesterol: 0
- Protein: 0.4
- Total Fat: 0.2
- Sodium: 15
- Total Carbohydrate: 62.5

41. Candied Apples III

Serving: 12 | Prep: 5mins | Ready in:

Ingredients

- 1 2/3 cups cinnamon red hot candies
- 2 tablespoons water
- 12 apples

Direction

- Stick craft sticks into apples. With waxed paper, line a baking sheet.
- Over medium-high heat, put water with candies in a heavy-bottomed saucepan. Brushing down sides of the pan from time to time with a heat-resistant pastry brush, cook candy to 300 to 310°F (149 to 154°C), or until a drop of syrup poured into cold water forms hard, brittle threads. Take off from heat and rest until slightly cool.
- Plunge apples in hot liquid and put on waxed paper to set.

Nutrition Information

- Calories: 189 calories;
- Sodium: 13
- Total Carbohydrate: 48.1
- Cholesterol: 0
- Protein: 0.4
- Total Fat: 0.2

42. Candied Sweet Potatoes

Serving: 5 | Prep: | Ready in:

Ingredients

- 2 sweet potatoes
- 1/4 cup butter
- 1/2 cup packed brown sugar
- 1/4 cup orange juice

Direction

- Boil cut-up sweet potatoes/bake whole sweet potatoes till tender at 175°C/350°F.
- Melt brown sugar and butter together till bubbly in a frying pan. Add orange juice; mix till smooth. Add cut-up sweet potatoes; slowly cook for 20 minutes till sweet potatoes caramelize, occasionally turning. Add a little more brown sugar if syrup is too thin.

Nutrition Information

- Calories: 215 calories;
- Sodium: 100
- Total Carbohydrate: 33.3
- Cholesterol: 24
- Protein: 1
- Total Fat: 9.3

43. Caprese Appetizer

Serving: 10 | Prep: 15mins | Ready in:

Ingredients

- 20 grape tomatoes
- 10 ounces mozzarella cheese, cubed
- 2 tablespoons extra virgin olive oil
- 2 tablespoons fresh basil leaves, chopped
- 1 pinch salt
- 1 pinch ground black pepper

- 20 toothpicks

Direction

- In a bowl, toss together mozzarella cheese, tomatoes, basil, olive oil, salt, and pepper until well coated. On each toothpick, create a skewer with one tomato and a piece of mozzarella cheese.

Nutrition Information

- Calories: 104 calories;
- Total Fat: 7.3
- Sodium: 179
- Total Carbohydrate: 2.4
- Cholesterol: 18
- Protein: 7.2

44. Carmel's Stuffing

Serving: 4 | Prep: 10mins | Ready in:

Ingredients

- 1 large carrot, grated
- 1 large onion, finely chopped
- 2 cups dry bread crumbs
- 3 teaspoons chopped fresh parsley
- 3 teaspoons fresh thyme
- 1 cup butter

Direction

- Mix together the thyme, parsley, bread crumbs, onion and carrot in a big bowl, then stir well.
- Melt the butter in a big saucepan on medium heat. Lower the heat and mix in the carrot mixture. Let it cook for about 15 minutes, stirring from time to time, until the mixture is heated through and the carrot and onion become tender.

Nutrition Information

- Calories: 643 calories;
- Cholesterol: 122
- Protein: 8.4
- Total Fat: 49
- Sodium: 730
- Total Carbohydrate: 44.1

45. Cheesy Broccoli Rice Casserole

Serving: 8 | Prep: 10mins | Ready in:

Ingredients

- 1 (8 ounce) package processed cheese, cubed
- 1 (10.75 ounce) can condensed cream of chicken soup
- 1 cup cooked wild rice
- 1 (10 ounce) package frozen chopped broccoli, thawed
- 1/2 cup chopped onion
- 1/2 cup chopped celery
- 1 dash hot sauce
- ground black pepper to taste
- 1 (2.8 ounce) can French-fried onions

Direction

- In a 2-quart microwave-safe casserole dish, place cheese; cook for 1 to 2 minutes until most of the cheese has melted. Add chicken soup, chopped onion, black pepper, wild rice, celery, hot sauce and broccoli and stir.
- Cook fully in a microwave for 12 to 14 minutes, rotate the dish mid-way. Spread French-fried onions over the casserole, leave it to cook for a minute more.

Nutrition Information

- Calories: 228 calories;
- Total Fat: 14.3
- Sodium: 628
- Total Carbohydrate: 16.7

- Cholesterol: 21
- Protein: 8.5

46. Cheesy Mashed Potatoes With Cubed Ham

Serving: 6 | Prep: 10mins | Ready in:

Ingredients

- 5 baking potatoes, peeled and cut into 1/2-inch cubes
- 1 cup butter
- 1 1/2 tablespoons garlic powder
- 1 tablespoon dried parsley
- 1 1/2 cups shredded Cheddar cheese
- 1 pound cubed cooked ham

Direction

- In a big pot, put potatoes and pour salted water over the potatoes to cover, boil. Lower the heat to medium-low and simmer until the potatoes become tender, approximately 20 minutes. Drain. Put the potatoes into a bowl; add parsley, garlic powder and butter. Use a potato masher to mash. Put in ham and Cheddar cheese and stir.

Nutrition Information

- Calories: 715 calories;
- Total Fat: 54.2
- Sodium: 1377
- Total Carbohydrate: 33.1
- Cholesterol: 153
- Protein: 25.3

47. Chef John's Easy Apple Pie

Serving: 8 | Prep: 30mins | Ready in:

Ingredients

- 6 tablespoons unsalted butter
- 1/4 cup white sugar
- 1/2 cup brown sugar
- 1 pinch salt
- 1/4 teaspoon ground cinnamon
- 1/4 cup water
- 1 (15 ounce) package double crust ready-to-use pie crust (such as Pillsbury®)
- 4 large red apples, cored and thinly sliced

Direction

- Set oven to 425 degrees Fahrenheit (220 degrees C).
- Using a pan, melt butter over medium heat and stir in water, cinnamon, salt, brown sugar, and white sugar. Allow the syrup to boil, constantly stirring until sugar dissolves, then take off the heat.
- Unroll the crusts and press one of them onto a 9 inches pie dish, then place apples in the crust. Unroll the other pie crust onto a work area and cut into 8 1-inch wide strips. Criss-cross the strips or weave into a lattice crust over the apples. Crimp the bottom crust over the strips using your fingers. Spoon the caramel sauce onto the pie to cover the lattice of the top crust and let the leftover sauce drizzle throughout the crust.
- Bake for 15 minutes in preheated oven, then bring down the heat to 350 degrees Fahrenheit (175 degrees C). Bake for 35-40 minutes more until the filling is bubbly, the crust turns golden brown, and the caramel is set. Let the pie completely cool before slicing.

Nutrition Information

- Calories: 454 calories;
- Protein: 3.4
- Total Fat: 25
- Sodium: 259
- Total Carbohydrate: 56.6
- Cholesterol: 23

48. Chef John's Perfect Mashed Potatoes

Serving: 4 | Prep: 20mins | Ready in:

Ingredients

- 3 large russet potatoes, peeled and cut in half lengthwise
- 1/4 cup butter
- 1/2 cup whole milk
- salt and ground black pepper to taste

Direction

- Add potatoes to the big pot, and cover with the salted water. Boil, lower the heat to medium-low, keep covered and let simmer for 20-25 minutes till soft. Drain off and bring potatoes back to pot. Switch the heat to high, and let potatoes dry for roughly half a minute. Switch off heat.
- Mash potatoes using the potato masher two times around pot, then put in milk and butter. Keep mashing till fluffy and smooth. Whisk in black pepper and salt for roughly 15 seconds till equally distributed.

Nutrition Information

- Calories: 333 calories;
- Protein: 6.7
- Total Fat: 12.7
- Sodium: 30
- Total Carbohydrate: 49.7
- Cholesterol: 34

49. Chicken Or Turkey Pot Pie

Serving: 8 | Prep: 10mins | Ready in:

Ingredients

- 2 prepared pie crusts
- 2 cups coarsely chopped leftover turkey
- 1 (16 ounce) package frozen vegetable blend, thawed
- 1 (10.75 ounce) can condensed cream of chicken soup
- 1/2 cup half and half, or to taste
- salt and ground black pepper to taste

Direction

- Preheat oven to 350° F (175° C). Line 1 prepared pie crust onto a pie plate.
- In a bowl, mix black pepper, salt, half-and-half, chicken soup, vegetables and turkey. Pour into prepared pie plate and put the leftover pie crust on top. Cut 4 slits in the top of the crust to vent.
- Bake in the preheated oven for 40-45 minutes until heated through and crust turns golden.

Nutrition Information

- Calories: 377 calories;
- Cholesterol: 35
- Protein: 16.3
- Total Fat: 20.9
- Sodium: 560
- Total Carbohydrate: 31.5

50. Chinese Style Peanut Cookie

Serving: 48 | Prep: 12mins | Ready in:

Ingredients

- 3/4 cup roasted peanuts, finely ground
- 1 cup all-purpose flour
- 1/4 cup corn flour
- 1 1/4 cups confectioners' sugar
- 1/2 cup vegetable oil
- 1 egg yolk, beaten (optional)

Direction

- Set the oven to 350°F (175°C) for preheating. Use parchment paper to line baking pans.
- In a large bowl, combine corn flour, confectioners' sugar, peanuts, and flour and mix them thoroughly. Make a hole in the center of the peanut mixture. Gradually pour vegetable oil into the hole. Mix the oil and peanut mixture to make a wet and slightly sticky dough. Take at least 2 teaspoons of dough and roll it to make a 1/2-inch diameter ball. Do the same with the remaining dough. Place the balls into the lined baking pans. You can coat each with egg yolk if you want.
- Bake the balls in the preheated oven for 6-8 minutes until the cookies are golden brown. Transfer the pan on racks to cool.

Nutrition Information

- Calories: 59 calories;
- Total Carbohydrate: 6.3
- Cholesterol: 4
- Protein: 0.9
- Total Fat: 3.5
- Sodium: 1

51. Chocolate Bar Hot Chocolate

Serving: 1 | Prep: 5mins | Ready in:

Ingredients

- 1 (1.55 ounce) bar milk chocolate candy bar, chopped
- 2/3 cup milk, or more to taste
- 1 pinch ground cinnamon (optional)

Direction

- In a saucepan, place chocolate pieces over medium-low heat. Pour in milk and constantly whisk for 5 minutes to melt and well blend the chocolate. Add in cinnamon and whisk. Take away from the heat and pour in more milk if preferred. Transfer into a mug to serve.

Nutrition Information

- Calories: 319 calories;
- Sodium: 102
- Total Carbohydrate: 34.6
- Cholesterol: 23
- Protein: 8.8
- Total Fat: 16.3

52. Chocolate Pumpkin Bundt® Cake

Serving: 16 | Prep: 10mins | Ready in:

Ingredients

- 1 (15.25 ounce) package chocolate cake mix
- 4 eggs
- 1 cup pumpkin puree
- 3/4 cup white sugar
- 1/2 cup oil
- 1/4 cup water
- 1/2 teaspoon ground cinnamon
- 1/2 teaspoon nutmeg

Direction

- Preheat an oven to 175°C or 350°F. Grease one fluted tube pan like Bundt(R) and dust with flour.
- In bowl, stir nutmeg, cinnamon, water, oil, sugar, pumpkin puree, eggs and chocolate cake mix; put to prepped pan.
- In prepped oven, bake for 35 to 45 minutes, till an inserted toothpick in the middle gets out clean.

Nutrition Information

- Calories: 236 calories;
- Sodium: 241
- Total Carbohydrate: 30.5
- Cholesterol: 46

- Protein: 3.4
- Total Fat: 12.4

53. Cindy's Turkey Salad

Serving: 12 | Prep: 15mins | Ready in:

Ingredients

- 5 cups cooked turkey meat, chopped
- 1 cup finely chopped celery
- 1 fresh jalapeno pepper, diced
- 3 tablespoons sweet pickle relish
- 1 cup mayonnaise
- 1 tablespoon dried cilantro
- 2 teaspoons salt
- 2 teaspoons pepper

Direction

- Mix together mayonnaise, relish, jalapeno, celery, and turkey meat in a bowl. Add salt, pepper and cilantro to season. Keep cold in refrigerator until serving.

Nutrition Information

- Calories: 239 calories;
- Sodium: 572
- Total Carbohydrate: 2.6
- Cholesterol: 51
- Protein: 17.4
- Total Fat: 17.5

54. Classic Savory Deviled Eggs

Serving: 6 | Prep: 10mins | Ready in:

Ingredients

- 6 hard-cooked eggs, halved
- 1/4 cup mayonnaise
- 1 teaspoon rice wine vinegar
- 1/2 teaspoon chopped fresh dill
- 1 teaspoon Dijon mustard
- 1/4 teaspoon garlic powder
- 1/8 teaspoon salt
- 12 sprigs fresh dill (optional)

Direction

- In a bowl, put the egg yolks and put the egg whites aside. Crush salt, garlic powder, Dijon mustard, 1/2 teaspoon of chopped dill, vinegar, mayonnaise, and the yolks together. Use the yolk mixture to put into each egg white. Use dill sprigs to garnish. Chill until ready to eat.

Nutrition Information

- Calories: 139 calories;
- Cholesterol: 189
- Protein: 6.4
- Total Fat: 12.3
- Sodium: 192
- Total Carbohydrate: 1

55. Cozy Mulled Wine

Serving: 6 | Prep: 10mins | Ready in:

Ingredients

- 1 (750 milliliter) bottle red wine (such as Cabernet Sauvignon, Zinfandel, or Merlot)
- 1 orange, peeled and sliced
- 2/3 cup honey
- 1/4 cup brandy
- 3 cinnamon sticks
- 8 whole cloves, or more to taste
- 1 teaspoon grated fresh ginger

Direction

- In a slow cooker, mix ginger, cloves, cinnamon sticks, brandy, honey, orange slices and red wine.
- Cook on Low for 20-25 minutes until wine is steaming.

Nutrition Information

- Calories: 256 calories;
- Total Carbohydrate: 35.9
- Cholesterol: 0
- Protein: 0.3
- Total Fat: 0.1
- Sodium: 10

56. Cranberry Apple Oatmeal

Serving: 2 | Prep: 10mins | Ready in:

Ingredients

- 2 cups water
- 1 apple, cored and diced
- 1/2 cup fresh cranberries
- 1 cup quick-cooking oats
- 1/4 cup brown sugar
- 1/2 teaspoon ground cinnamon
- 1/4 teaspoon ground nutmeg
- 1 pinch salt
- 1/2 cup chopped walnuts

Direction

- In a bowl, bring the mixture of cranberries, apple and water to a boil. Cook about 5 minutes until apple is soft and cranberries burst. Lower heat to medium and stir in salt, nutmeg, cinnamon, brown sugar and oats. Cook and stir constantly for 2-3 minutes, until oatmeal absorbs water and thickens. Garnish with walnuts on top.

Nutrition Information

- Calories: 499 calories;
- Sodium: 19
- Total Carbohydrate: 71.5
- Cholesterol: 0
- Protein: 10.1
- Total Fat: 22

57. Cranberry Gravy

Serving: 8 | Prep: 10mins | Ready in:

Ingredients

- 1/4 cup water
- 1 tablespoon cornstarch
- 1 1/2 cups cranberry sauce
- 1/2 cup turkey drippings
- 2 teaspoons curry powder
- 1 teaspoon thyme
- 1 teaspoon anise seed
- 1 teaspoon ground cardamom
- 1 teaspoon orange zest

Direction

- Whisk cornstarch and water till smooth in a bowl.
- Cook orange zest, cardamom, anise seed, thyme, curry powder, turkey drippings and cranberry sauce for 5 minutes in a small saucepan over medium heat, occasionally mixing.
- Mix cornstarch mixture to get rid of lumps; put into the cranberry mixture. Lower heat to medium low; cook for 5-10 minutes till gravy is thick, occasionally mixing.

Nutrition Information

- Calories: 198 calories;
- Sodium: 12
- Total Carbohydrate: 21.2
- Cholesterol: 13
- Protein: 0.2

- Total Fat: 12.9

58. Cranberry Jalapeno Cream Cheese Dip

Serving: 16 | Prep: 10mins | Ready in:

Ingredients

- 1/4 cup vegetable oil
- 10 ounces dried sweetened cranberries
- 1/2 cup white sugar, or to taste
- 1/2 cup water, or more as needed
- 2 small jalapeno peppers, seeded and finely diced
- 1 tablespoon lemon juice
- 2 teaspoons dried cilantro
- 1/4 teaspoon salt
- 2 (8 ounce) packages cream cheese, softened

Direction

- Heat the saucepan on medium heat; pour in the oil. Whisk the cranberries in the hot oil and cook for 5-10 minutes or till most of the oil is absorbed by the cranberries. Stir the salt, cilantro, lemon juice, jalapeno peppers, water and sugar to the cranberries; cook for 10-15 minutes longer or till reduced and tender. Pour in additional water if necessary.
- Puree the cranberry mixture in the food processor/blender till very smooth; let cool down totally.
- Whisk together the cream cheese and cooled cranberry mixture in the bowl till creamy and smooth.

Nutrition Information

- Calories: 205 calories;
- Total Fat: 13.2
- Sodium: 120
- Total Carbohydrate: 21.7
- Cholesterol: 31

- Protein: 2.2

59. Cranberry Pecan Cake

Serving: 12 | Prep: 20mins | Ready in:

Ingredients

- 3 cups frozen cranberries
- 1 cup pecans
- 1 cup white sugar
- 2 eggs
- 1 cup white sugar
- 1 cup all-purpose flour
- 1/2 cup butter, melted
- 2 tablespoons milk

Direction

- Preheat the oven to 175 degrees C (350 degrees F). Liberally grease the 2-qt. rectangular baking dish.
- Spread cranberries equally on bottom of baking dish, and drizzle pecans on cranberries. Scoop 1 cup of the sugar on pecans and cranberries.
- Add eggs to the working bowl of the electric mixer, and whip on high speed till eggs become foamy or for roughly 60 seconds. Whip in milk, melted butter, flour and 1 cup of the sugar on Low speed till just mixed. Batter should be thick. Spread batter equally on pecan-cranberry mixture.
- Bake in preheated oven for 40-45 minutes or till cake turns lightly brown and the toothpick inserted near the middle comes out clean. Gently invert cake onto the serving dish, so the pecan-cranberry layer is on the top. Allow it to cool down for half an hour prior to serving.

Nutrition Information

- Calories: 327 calories;
- Total Carbohydrate: 45.7

- Cholesterol: 52
- Protein: 3.3
- Total Fat: 15.8
- Sodium: 68

60. Cranberry Stuffed Turkey Breasts

Serving: 10 | Prep: 45mins | Ready in:

Ingredients

- 1 (12 ounce) package herb-seasoned bread stuffing mix
- 2 skinless boneless turkey breasts
- 1 cup chopped pecans
- 2 (8 ounce) packages dried, sweetened cranberries
- 2 tablespoons olive oil
- 6 lettuce leaves
- 1/2 cup pecan halves

Direction

- Set the oven to 350°F (175°C) for preheating. Follow the package directions on how to prepare the stuffing. Put the stuffing aside to cool.
- Use a sharp knife to butterfly open the breast for it to lay flat. Position each breast between the 2 sheets of waxed paper. Use a mallet to flatten the breast. Pour the prepared stuffing to within 1/4-inch of the edges of the breasts. Sprinkle each breast with dried cranberries and chopped pecans, reserving some of cranberries for the garnish. Roll the breast up tightly like a jellyroll style, making sure to start rolling with the long end. Tuck the ends of the roll and tie the rolls in sections using the string, about 4 sections around the center and 1 section running the length of the roll so that the ends are tightly secured.
- Put olive oil in a large cast-iron skillet and heat it over medium-high heat. Brown all the sides of the rolls carefully.
- Place the uncovered skillet inside the oven. Let the rolls bake inside the preheated oven for 1 hour or until their internal temperature reaches 170°F (78°C) when measured using a meat thermometer. Don't let the rolls get overly dry.
- Let the rolls set for 15 minutes before taking the string away. Slice the rolls into 1/2-3/4-inch circles. Cut the other roll for a nice presentation and leave one roll whole. The stuffing will be spiraled into the meat. Decorate the slices nicely on a platter with a bed of curly lettuce. Garnish the serving platter with the reserved dried cranberries and the remaining half cup of the pecan halves.

Nutrition Information

- Calories: 369 calories;
- Sodium: 858
- Total Carbohydrate: 28
- Cholesterol: 34
- Protein: 23.2
- Total Fat: 18.4

61. Cream Cheese Snowball Cookies

Serving: 24 | Prep: 23mins | Ready in:

Ingredients

- 1 cup confectioners' sugar
- 1/2 cup finely-chopped walnuts (optional)
- 1/2 cup vegetable shortening (such as Crisco®)
- 1/2 cup butter, softened
- 1/2 cup cream cheese, softened
- 1/2 cup white sugar
- 1/2 teaspoon almond extract
- 1/2 teaspoon vanilla extract
- 1 1/2 cups all-purpose flour

Direction

- Preheat the oven to 350°F (175°C). In a shallow bowl, sift the confectioners' sugar, mix in walnuts, and put aside.
- In a bowl, beat sugar, cream cheese, butter and shortening together until the mixture is creamy and completely blended. Add in flour, vanilla extract and almond extract and stir until combined. Scoop the dough up by rounded tablespoons, and roll into 1-in. balls in diameter. On ungreased baking sheets, arrange the balls approximately 1 1/2 inches apart.
- Bake in the preheated oven in about 6 minutes, until the edges are slightly golden. Cool the cookies in about 1 minute on the baking sheets, then roll in confectioners' sugar-and-walnut mixture while the cookies are still a little bit warm.

Nutrition Information

- Calories: 170 calories;
- Total Fat: 11.5
- Sodium: 42
- Total Carbohydrate: 15.8
- Cholesterol: 15
- Protein: 1.6

62. Cream Corn Like No Other

Serving: 8 | Prep: 5mins | Ready in:

Ingredients

- 2 (10 ounce) packages frozen corn kernels, thawed
- 1 cup heavy cream
- 1 teaspoon salt
- 2 tablespoons granulated sugar
- 1/4 teaspoon freshly ground black pepper
- 2 tablespoons butter
- 1 cup whole milk
- 2 tablespoons all-purpose flour
- 1/4 cup freshly grated Parmesan cheese

Direction

- Mix together butter, pepper, sugar, salt, cream and corn in a skillet on moderate heat. Whisk flour and milk together, then stir into the corn mixture. Cook and stir on moderate heat until corn is cooked through and the mixture thickens. Take away from the heat and stir in Parmesan cheese until it is melted. Serve hot.

Nutrition Information

- Calories: 253 calories;
- Cholesterol: 54
- Protein: 5.1
- Total Fat: 16.5
- Sodium: 373
- Total Carbohydrate: 24.8

63. Creamy Pumpkin Spice Martini

Serving: 1 | Prep: 5mins | Ready in:

Ingredients

- 1 cup ice cubes, or as desired
- 2 fluid ounces pumpkin liqueur
- 2 fluid ounces apple cider
- 1 fluid ounce spiced rum
- 1 tablespoon half-and-half
- 1 tablespoon whipped cream, or to taste
- 1 pinch ground nutmeg

Direction

- Fill ice in the shaker. Add half-and-half, spiced rum, apple cider and pumpkin liqueur. Cover and shake till it is frosty on the outside of the shaker. In a martini glass, pour drink and use nutmeg and whipped cream to garnish.

Nutrition Information

- Calories: 326 calories;

- Total Carbohydrate: 34
- Cholesterol: 8
- Protein: 0.6
- Total Fat: 2.9
- Sodium: 28

64. Curried Carrot Soup

Serving: 6 | Prep: 15mins | Ready in:

Ingredients

- 2 tablespoons vegetable oil
- 1 onion, chopped
- 1 tablespoon curry powder
- 2 pounds carrots, chopped
- 4 cups vegetable broth
- 2 cups water, or as needed

Direction

- In a large pot placed over medium heat, pour the oil. Sauté onion until it becomes transparent and soft. Introduce the chopped carrots and curry powder; stir until the carrots are coated. Add the vegetable broth and let simmer for 20 minutes, until the carrots are tender.
- Blend the carrots and broth in a blender; ensuring it becomes smooth. Transfer back to the pot, and dilute with water until it reaches your desired consistency.

Nutrition Information

- Calories: 133 calories;
- Cholesterol: 0
- Protein: 2.4
- Total Fat: 5.4
- Sodium: 415
- Total Carbohydrate: 20.2

65. Deborah's Holiday Mashed Potatoes

Serving: 10 | Prep: 15mins | Ready in:

Ingredients

- 6 white potatoes, diced
- 1/2 cup sour cream
- 1/4 cup milk
- 1/4 cup butter
- 1/4 cup finely diced jalapeno pepper, or to taste
- 1/4 cup shredded Monterey Jack cheese
- 1 tablespoon garlic powder

Direction

- Cover potatoes with salted water in a large pot; bring to a boil. Turn heat to medium-low; simmer for about 20 to 25 minutes until soft. Drain off water.
- In a bowl, mash potatoes with garlic powder, Monterey Jack cheese, jalapeno pepper, butter, milk, and sour cream with a fork or potato masher until well combined and no lumps remain.

Nutrition Information

- Calories: 181 calories;
- Total Fat: 8.1
- Sodium: 32
- Total Carbohydrate: 23.9
- Cholesterol: 20
- Protein: 4.1

66. Delicious Cinnamon Baked Apples

Serving: 6 | Prep: 15mins | Ready in:

Ingredients

- 1 teaspoon butter
- 2 tablespoons brown sugar
- 3 teaspoons vanilla sugar
- 3 teaspoons ground cinnamon
- 1 teaspoon ground nutmeg
- 6 large apples - peeled, cored, and sliced
- 3 1/2 tablespoons water

Direction

- Set oven to 350 0F (175 0 C) and preheat. Coat a large baking dish using the butter.
- In a small bowl, combine nutmeg, cinnamon, vanilla sugar and brown sugar. Lay about 1/3 of the apples in the buttered baking dish; sprinkle over the apples with 1/3 of the sugar mixture. Repeat layers two more times.
- Put in the prepared oven and bake for 30 minutes. Pour water over apples and keep baking for about 15 minutes longer until tender.

Nutrition Information

- Calories: 147 calories;
- Total Carbohydrate: 37
- Cholesterol: 2
- Protein: 0.6
- Total Fat: 1.2
- Sodium: 9

67. Delicious Vegan Hot Chocolate

Serving: 2 | Prep: 5mins | Ready in:

Ingredients

- 2 1/2 cups soy milk
- 3 tablespoons white sugar
- 3 tablespoons cocoa powder
- 1/2 teaspoon salt
- 1/2 teaspoon vanilla extract
- 1 pinch ground cinnamon
- 1 pinch cayenne pepper

Direction

- In a saucepan, bring cayenne pepper, cinnamon, vanilla extract, salt, cocoa powder, sugar and soy milk to a simmer over medium-high heat. Take away from the heat then whisk till frothy. Immediately serve.

Nutrition Information

- Calories: 259 calories;
- Total Carbohydrate: 42.9
- Cholesterol: 0
- Protein: 11.4
- Total Fat: 6.4
- Sodium: 738

68. Deviled Egg Appetizer Dip

Serving: 24 | Prep: 20mins | Ready in:

Ingredients

- 12 eggs
- 1 cup mayonnaise
- 1 tablespoon Dijon mustard
- 2 tablespoons white wine vinegar
- 1 teaspoon red hot sauce

Direction

- Put the eggs in a pan and cover them with water, then boil. Take away from the heat and allow the eggs to cook in the hot water without the heat for 12 minutes. Pour out the hot water and place the eggs in a bowl with ice water for them to cool.
- Peel the eggs and cut in half. Cut 1/2 of the egg whites and place in a bowl.
- Place the yolks and leftover egg whites in a food processor with hot sauce, white wine vinegar, Dijon mustard, and mayonnaise, process until smooth and move to a bowl. Fold in the chopped egg whites and serve.

Nutrition Information

- Calories: 98 calories;
- Total Carbohydrate: 0.6
- Cholesterol: 85
- Protein: 2.9
- Total Fat: 9.5
- Sodium: 104

69. Deviled Eggs I

Serving: 6 | Prep: 20mins | Ready in:

Ingredients

- 6 eggs
- 1/2 teaspoon paprika
- 2 tablespoons mayonnaise
- 1/2 teaspoon mustard powder

Direction

- In a pot, put eggs with salted water. Boil the water, allow the eggs to cook in the boiling water for about 10-15 minutes until they are hard boiled. Strain the eggs and let cool down.
- Slice the eggs into two lengthwise. Scoop the yolks into a small mixing bowl and crush them together. Stir in dry mustard, mayonnaise, and paprika. Use the mixture to put into each egg white; cool and enjoy.

Nutrition Information

- Calories: 107 calories;
- Protein: 6.4
- Total Fat: 8.7
- Sodium: 96
- Total Carbohydrate: 0.7
- Cholesterol: 188

70. Easy Apple Crisp

Serving: 12 | Prep: | Ready in:

Ingredients

- 6 apple - peeled, cored and sliced
- 1 cup water
- 1 (18.25 ounce) package white cake mix
- 1 cup packed brown sugar
- 1 teaspoon ground cinnamon
- 1/2 cup butter, melted

Direction

- Prepare the oven by preheating to 350°F (175°C). Prepare a 9x13-inch baking dish that is lightly greased.
- At the bottom of a baking dish, place apples in an equal layer. Put water on apples.
- Combine cinnamon, brown sugar, and cake mix in a medium bowl. Mix in melted butter or margarine until ingredients are well mixed; you will have a crumbly mixture. Dust mixture on apples.
- Place in the preheated oven and bake for 50-55 minutes.

Nutrition Information

- Calories: 355 calories;
- Total Fat: 12.4
- Sodium: 344
- Total Carbohydrate: 60.9
- Cholesterol: 20
- Protein: 2.2

71. Easy Awesome Shrimp Scampi

Serving: 8 | Prep: 10mins | Ready in:

Ingredients

- 1 cup butter
- 1 pound cooked small salad shrimp

- 2 sleeves buttery round crackers (such as Ritz®), crushed
- 3 tablespoons lemon juice
- 4 teaspoons garlic powder

Direction

- Set the oven at 250°F (120°C) and start preheating.
- In a saucepan over medium heat, melt butter. Fold shrimp into the melted butter to coat properly. Stir in garlic powder, lemon juice and cracker crumbs; remove into a 9-in. square baking dish. Use aluminum foil to cover the dish.
- Bake for around 45 minutes in the preheated oven, or till bubbling.

Nutrition Information

- Calories: 410 calories;
- Sodium: 547
- Total Carbohydrate: 18
- Cholesterol: 172
- Protein: 14
- Total Fat: 31.5

72. Easy Baked Pumpkin Pudding

Serving: 10 | Prep: 10mins | Ready in:

Ingredients

- 1/4 cup butter, melted
- 2 cups pumpkin puree
- 1 cup white sugar
- 1 cup evaporated milk
- 1/2 cup all-purpose flour
- 2 eggs, beaten
- 1 tablespoon vanilla extract
- 1/2 teaspoon salt
- 1 pinch baking soda
- 1/2 cup white sugar
- 2 tablespoons ground cinnamon

Direction

- Preheat the oven to 230 degrees C (450 degrees F). Add the melted butter to a 2-qt. baking plate.
- Stir the baking soda, salt, vanilla extract, eggs, flour, evaporated milk, 1 cup of the sugar and pumpkin in a big bowl; add to prepped baking plate. Mix the cinnamon and leftover half cup of the sugar in a small-sized bowl; dust on the pumpkin mixture.
- Bake in preheated oven for roughly half an hour till the middle becomes set.

Nutrition Information

- Calories: 251 calories;
- Sodium: 336
- Total Carbohydrate: 42.6
- Cholesterol: 57
- Protein: 4.3
- Total Fat: 7.7

73. Easy Corn Pudding

Serving: 6 | Prep: | Ready in:

Ingredients

- 1 (15 ounce) can creamed corn
- 1 (15.25 ounce) can whole kernel corn
- 1/4 pound butter, softened
- 1 (8.5 ounce) package corn bread mix
- 1 (8 ounce) container sour cream (optional)

Direction

- Set oven to 350°F (175°C) to preheat. Place butter in a 2-quart casserole dish; put the dish into the heated oven to melt butter.
- Take the dish out of the oven and add sour cream, corn muffin mix, kernel corn, and creamed corn. Stir thoroughly. Bake without covering for about half an hour in the preheated oven.

Nutrition Information

- Calories: 486 calories;
- Sodium: 1209
- Total Carbohydrate: 56.1
- Cholesterol: 58
- Protein: 7.8
- Total Fat: 28.1

74. Easy Cranberry Orange Relish

Serving: 8 | Prep: 10mins | Ready in:

Ingredients

- 1 navel orange
- 1 (12 ounce) package fresh cranberries
- 1/2 cup white sugar
- 1/8 teaspoon ground cinnamon

Direction

- Grate 2 teaspoons of orange zest and discard the remaining peel and pith from the orange. Divide into sections.
- In a food processor, place cinnamon, sugar, cranberries, orange zest, and orange sections, then pulse until chopped finely.
- Transfer relish into a bowl, cover, then refrigerate for at least 2 hours so the flavors blend.

Nutrition Information

- Calories: 76 calories;
- Total Fat: 0.1
- Sodium: 1
- Total Carbohydrate: 19.8
- Cholesterol: 0
- Protein: 0.3

75. Easy Cranberry Raspberry Sauce

Serving: 24 | Prep: 5mins | Ready in:

Ingredients

- 2 (12 ounce) jars seedless raspberry jam
- 2 (12 ounce) packages fresh cranberries
- 1 teaspoon ground cinnamon
- 1/2 teaspoon ground allspice
- 2 teaspoons lemon zest

Direction

- In a saucepan, heat jam on moderate heat, then put in allspice, cinnamon and cranberries. Lower heat to moderately low, then cook for 10-15 minutes while stirring often, until cranberries start to pop. Take away from the heat then stir in lemon zest. Chill for a minimum of an hour to let thicken before serving.

Nutrition Information

- Calories: 84 calories;
- Total Fat: 0
- Sodium: 1
- Total Carbohydrate: 21.8
- Cholesterol: 0
- Protein: 0.1

76. Easy Crustless Pumpkin Pie

Serving: 8 | Prep: 10mins | Ready in:

Ingredients

- 1 (15 ounce) can pumpkin puree
- 1 1/4 cups skim milk
- 3/4 cup granular sucralose sweetener (such as Splenda®)
- 1/2 cup egg substitute
- 1 teaspoon vanilla extract

- 1 teaspoon ground cinnamon
- 1/2 teaspoon ground ginger
- 1/2 teaspoon ground nutmeg

Direction

- Preheat the oven to 175°C or 350°F. Oil a pie dish.
- In a bowl, whisk nutmeg, ginger, cinnamon, vanilla extract, egg substitute, sweetener, milk and pumpkin puree till smooth; put into prepped pie dish.
- In preheated oven, bake for about half an hour till firm.

Nutrition Information

- Calories: 48 calories;
- Sodium: 172
- Total Carbohydrate: 6.8
- Cholesterol: 1
- Protein: 3.8
- Total Fat: 0.8

77. Easy Garden Green Beans

Serving: 4 | Prep: 10mins | Ready in:

Ingredients

- 1 pound fresh green beans, trimmed
- 3 tablespoons olive oil
- 3 cloves garlic, sliced
- 1 pinch salt
- 1 pinch ground black pepper
- 2 tablespoons white wine vinegar
- 3 tablespoons freshly grated Parmesan cheese
- 2 tablespoons chopped fresh parsley

Direction

- Insert a steamer basket into a big saucepan and pour in water until just beneath the steamer. Boil it. Add green beans, and steam for 5 minutes, until reaching your wanted softness.
- When the beans have cooked, remove them into a serving bowl. Toss with Parmesan cheese, white wine vinegar, pepper, salt, garlic, and olive oil. Let sit for 10 minutes. Discard garlic slices and use parsley to garnish before eating.

Nutrition Information

- Calories: 146 calories;
- Protein: 3.7
- Total Fat: 11.4
- Sodium: 67
- Total Carbohydrate: 9.3
- Cholesterol: 3

78. Easy Gravy

Serving: 8 | Prep: | Ready in:

Ingredients

- 1 tablespoon pareve margarine
- 1/4 cup all-purpose flour
- 3 cups vegetable broth
- 2 tablespoons miso paste
- 2 tablespoons warm water
- 2 teaspoons soy sauce
- 1/4 teaspoon onion powder

Direction

- Mix warm water and miso together in a small bowl; mix till miso has dissolved.
- Liquefy margarine over medium heat in a 2-quart saucepan. Mix in flour till dissolved. Put in onion powder, soy sauce, miso mixture and vegetable broth. Cook, mixing till thickened, over medium heat.

Nutrition Information

- Calories: 47 calories;
- Total Fat: 1.8
- Sodium: 424
- Total Carbohydrate: 6.2
- Cholesterol: 0
- Protein: 1.4

- Calories: 107 calories;
- Total Fat: 0.1
- Sodium: 11
- Total Carbohydrate: 27.6
- Cholesterol: 0
- Protein: 0.2

79. Easy Instant Pot® Cranberry Sauce

Serving: 16 | Prep: 5mins | Ready in:

Ingredients

- 1 1/2 pounds fresh cranberries
- 1 3/4 cups white sugar
- 1/4 cup orange juice
- 2 teaspoons grated orange zest
- 1 pinch salt
- 1 cinnamon stick

Direction

- In a multi-functional pressure cooker (like the Instant Pot®), mix orange zest, sugar, salt, orange juice, and cranberries. Cover with a lid then lock. Refer to the manufacturer's instructions to set the cooker in high pressure. Set the timer for 5 minutes. Let the pressure build for about 10 to 15 minutes. Refer to the manufacturer's instructions on how to release the pressure with the natural-release method for about 10 to 40 minutes. Unlock then uncover. Mix in the cinnamon stick and set the function to "Sauté."
- Leave to cook for 5 to 10 minutes or until the sauce thickens. Take out and discard the cinnamon stick then blend sauce into an immersion blender for a smoother consistency. Leave to cool. Sauce will continue to naturally thicken.

Nutrition Information

80. Easy Leftover Thanksgiving Turkey Pot Pie

Serving: 6 | Prep: 15mins | Ready in:

Ingredients

- 2 1/2 cups chopped cooked turkey
- 1 (10.75 ounce) can condensed cream of chicken soup
- 1 (15.5 ounce) can whole kernel corn, drained
- 1 (14.5 ounce) can sliced carrots, drained
- 1 (15 ounce) can sliced white potatoes, drained and chopped
- 1/4 cup chicken stock
- salt and ground black pepper to taste
- 2 1/4 cups biscuit baking mix (such as Bisquick®)
- 2/3 cup milk

Direction

- Set oven to 400 0 F (200 0 C) and preheat. Coat a 9x11-inch baking dish with grease.
- Gently mix chicken stock, potatoes, carrots, corn, cream of chicken soup and the cooked turkey together in a large bowl until thoroughly combined. Use black pepper and salt to season to taste. Move the mixture to the greased baking dish. In a second bowl, mix milk and the baking mix to shape a dough; roll the dough out to a 9x12-inch rectangle on a work surface sprinkled with flour. Put the dough on top of the baking dish.
- Put in the prepared oven and bake for about 25 minutes until the biscuit dough topping is browned and the filling is bubbling.

Nutrition Information

- Calories: 449 calories;
- Protein: 25.6
- Total Fat: 14
- Sodium: 1518
- Total Carbohydrate: 57.1
- Cholesterol: 51

81. Easy Orange Cranberry Glaze

Serving: 30 | Prep: 5mins | Ready in:

Ingredients

- 1 cup orange juice
- 1 cup packed dark brown sugar
- 1 (16 ounce) can jellied cranberry sauce
- 1 (3 inch) cinnamon stick

Direction

- In a saucepan, combine cranberry sauce, brown sugar and orange juice, then mix until the sugar dissolves. Let the mixture boil, then drop in the cinnamon stick and lower the heat to simmer. Let it cook for about 10 minutes, mixing often, until the glaze becomes bubbly and hot and the cranberry sauce melts.
- To you use this: During the final 45 minutes of cooking, brush the glaze all over roasted turkey. Put the turkey back into the oven and let it bake for 10-15 minutes to let the glaze set. Redo the process a few more times prior to the end of cooking process.

Nutrition Information

- Calories: 54 calories;
- Total Carbohydrate: 14
- Cholesterol: 0
- Protein: 0.1
- Total Fat: 0
- Sodium: 6

82. Easy Pleasy Mac N Cheesy US Navy Style

Serving: 6 | Prep: 15mins | Ready in:

Ingredients

- 8 ounces elbow macaroni
- 8 ounces processed cheese (such as Velveeta®), cubed
- 1 (10.75 ounce) can condensed Cheddar cheese soup
- 1 cup sour cream
- 1/4 cup freshly shredded Parmesan cheese
- 1/2 cup milk
- salt and ground black pepper to taste
- 1/2 cup crushed saltine crackers
- 2 tablespoons butter, melted

Direction

- Prepare the oven by preheating to 350°F (175°C). Prepare an 8x8-inch baking dish and grease.
- Put a lightly salted water in a large pot over high heat and make it to a rolling boil. When the water is boiling, add in the macaroni, and bring back to a boil. Cook the pasta, without cover, for about 8 minutes, stirring occasionally, until the pasta has cooked through, yet still firm to chew. Place in a colander set in the sink to drain well. Put the macaroni to a large bowl, and add in the black pepper, salt, milk, Parmesan cheese, sour cream, Cheddar cheese soup, and processed cheese cubes. Place into the prepared baking dish. Combine the cracker crumbs with the butter, and dust over the casserole. Use aluminum foil to cover the casserole.
- Place in the preheated oven and bake for about 30 minutes until bubbling; take off foil and bake for 5-10 more minutes until crumbs are golden brown in color.

Nutrition Information

- Calories: 447 calories;
- Cholesterol: 58
- Protein: 18
- Total Fat: 22.4
- Sodium: 1143
- Total Carbohydrate: 43.2

83. Easy Pumpkin Cream Trifle

Serving: 20 | Prep: 25mins | Ready in:

Ingredients

- 1 (18.25 ounce) package spice cake mix
- 1 (3.4 ounce) package instant vanilla pudding
- 1 cup pumpkin puree
- 1/2 cup water
- 1/2 cup vegetable oil
- 3 eggs
- 2 teaspoons pumpkin pie spice
- 2 cups cold milk
- 2 (3.4 ounce) packages cheesecake flavor instant pudding and pie filling
- 2 cups whipped topping
- 1 cup chopped toasted pecans
- 1 cup English toffee bits

Direction

- Preheat an oven to 175°C/350°F; grease 9x13-in. baking dish lightly.
- Mix pie spice, eggs, oil, water, pumpkin, vanilla pudding mix and cake mix in big mixing bowl; put in prepped dish.
- In heated oven, bake for 45-50 minutes. Cool on wire rack at room temperature; cut cake to 1-in. cubes.
- Whisk cheesecake pudding mix and milk; set for 2 minutes. Fold whipped topping into pudding mixture.
- Layer 1/3 cake cubes on bottom of big bowl; top using 1/3 cream mixture. Sprinkle 1/3 toffee bit and pecans. Repeat layers till you use all ingredients. Refrigerate before serving for 1 hour.

Nutrition Information

- Calories: 378 calories;
- Sodium: 423
- Total Carbohydrate: 42.7
- Cholesterol: 40
- Protein: 4.5
- Total Fat: 21.5

84. Easy Pumpkin Pancakes

Serving: 10 | Prep: 10mins | Ready in:

Ingredients

- 1 cup pumpkin pie filling
- 2 eggs
- 2 cups milk
- 2 cups all-purpose flour
- 4 teaspoons baking powder
- 1 tablespoon white sugar
- 1 teaspoon pumpkin pie spice
- 1 teaspoon ground cinnamon
- 1 pinch ground nutmeg

Direction

- In a bowl, whisk the eggs and pumpkin pie filling together until it becomes smooth. Add nutmeg, cinnamon, pumpkin pie spice, sugar, baking powder, flour and milk, then whisk until the batter becomes smooth.
- Heat a griddle that's lightly oiled on medium-high heat. Drop the batter on the griddle by big spoonfuls and let it cook for 3-4 minutes, until it is dry on the edges and bubbles are formed. Turn and let it cook for 2-3 minutes, until the other side turns brown. Redo the process with the leftover batter.

Nutrition Information

- Calories: 165 calories;

- Total Fat: 2.3
- Sodium: 286
- Total Carbohydrate: 30.7
- Cholesterol: 41
- Protein: 5.8

85. Easy Pumpkin Pie Smoothie

Serving: 4 | Prep: 10mins | Ready in:

Ingredients

- 12 ounces vanilla-flavored almond milk
- 8 ounces frozen pumpkin puree
- 1 cup ice cubes
- 1 banana
- 1/2 cup brown sugar
- 1 cinnamon graham cracker, crushed and divided
- 2 teaspoons wheat germ
- 1 teaspoon vanilla extract
- 1 teaspoon pumpkin pie spice
- 1/2 teaspoon ground cinnamon

Direction

- in a blender, blend together almond milk, wheat germ, pumpkin, ice cubes, pumpkin pie spice, banana, brown sugar, cinnamon, 1/2 the crushed cinnamon graham cracker, and vanilla until smooth. Stud individual servings with the rest of the graham cracker crumbs.

Nutrition Information

- Calories: 172 calories;
- Total Fat: 1.7
- Sodium: 220
- Total Carbohydrate: 39
- Cholesterol: 0
- Protein: 1.9

86. Easy Pumpkin Turnovers

Serving: 18 | Prep: 30mins | Ready in:

Ingredients

- 1 cup canned pumpkin
- 1/4 cup brown sugar
- 2 teaspoons ground cinnamon
- 2 teaspoons pumpkin pie spice
- 2 sheets frozen puff pastry, thawed

Direction

- Set the oven to 175°C or 350°F. Take 2 baking sheets and line them with parchment paper.
- In a bowl, combine pumpkin pie spice, pumpkin, cinnamon, and brown sugar.
- Roll the puff pastry out into a 12-in by 12-in square and cut nine 4-in squares out of each sheet.
- Using a spoon to proportion and place the pumpkin mixture in the middle of the pastry squares; dab water on the square's edges then fold from corner to cover. Secure by pinching the edges together; arrange on the parchment-lined baking sheets.
- Bake for 15mins in the preheated oven until the pastry is golden brown and puffed. Let cool for 10mins on the pans then move to a wire rack; completely cool.

Nutrition Information

- Calories: 165 calories;
- Total Fat: 10.3
- Sodium: 100
- Total Carbohydrate: 16.5
- Cholesterol: 0
- Protein: 2.1

87. Easy Sausage Cheese Balls

Serving: 36 | Prep: 10mins | Ready in:

Ingredients

- 1 pound sausage
- 4 cups shredded Cheddar cheese
- 3 cups baking mix

Direction

- Set the oven to 200°C or 400°F.
- Mix together dry baking mix, cheese and sausage in a medium size bowl, then shape the mixture into walnut-sized balls. Put on a cookie sheet lined with foil
- Bake for 12-15 minutes. Serve hot.

Nutrition Information

- Calories: 137 calories;
- Total Fat: 9.4
- Sodium: 354
- Total Carbohydrate: 7.5
- Cholesterol: 22
- Protein: 5.5

88. Easy Slow Cooker Squash

Serving: 6 | Prep: 10mins | Ready in:

Ingredients

- 4 pounds yellow summer squash, sliced
- 1 small onion, chopped
- 1/4 cup butter, cubed
- 1/4 pound processed cheese food (such as Velveeta®), cubed

Direction

- Cover onion and squash with enough water in a pot. Boil; cover. Simmer veggies for 10 minutes till tender; don't mix. Drain onion and squash in colander in sink.
- Layer cheese food cubes, butter cubes, cooked onions and squash gently in slow cooker. Put cooker on low; cook for 1 hour till cheese and butter makes creamy sauce and squash is very tender. Don't mix.

Nutrition Information

- Calories: 183 calories;
- Protein: 7.4
- Total Fat: 13
- Sodium: 300
- Total Carbohydrate: 12.7
- Cholesterol: 35

89. Easy Smoked Turkey

Serving: 12 | Prep: 20mins | Ready in:

Ingredients

- 1 (12 pound) thawed whole turkey, neck and giblets removed
- 1 tablespoon chopped fresh savory
- 1 tablespoon chopped fresh sage
- 1 tablespoon salt (optional)
- 1 tablespoon ground black pepper
- 1/8 cup olive oil
- 1/2 cup water

Direction

- Wash turkey and using paper towels, pat it dry. In a bowl, mix black pepper, salt, sage and savory; massage 1/2 of herb mix on the inside of turkey's cavity and neck cavity. Loosen turkey skin on legs and breast; massage the leftover 1/2 of herb mixture beneath the loosened skin. Massage the olive oil all over the turkey.
- Light 20 charcoal briquettes and on lower grate of kettle charcoal grill, put 1/2 of them on every side. Put a disposable aluminum baking pan or drip pan in the center of lower grate and add water. Once coals turn gray with ash, put a 2-inch square piece of hickory or different hardwood onto every coals' bank.

- Over cooking grate, put the turkey and place cover on grill. Using grill thermometer, check the temperature to keep heat between 65 to 120°C or 150 and 250°F; put in about 3 to 5 coals to every side approximately every 1 1/2 hours. Once hardwood pieces burn away, put in additional to maintain a consistent stream of smoke rising from wood. In case open flames erupt once you open the lid, extinguish them with a drizzle of beer or water.
- Let the turkey smoke for approximately 4 hours total, 20 minutes each pound; allow the temperature to raise to 120°C or 250°F on the final hour of smoking. An inserted instant-read meat thermometer into the chunkiest part of a thigh without touching bone should register 75°C or 165°F.

Nutrition Information

- Calories: 692 calories;
- Protein: 90.7
- Total Fat: 33.7
- Sodium: 801
- Total Carbohydrate: 0.4
- Cholesterol: 264

90. Easy Southern Sweet Potato Casserole

Serving: 8 | Prep: 10mins | Ready in:

Ingredients

- 1 pound sweet potatoes, peeled and cubed
- 1 cup brown sugar
- 1 (10.5 ounce) package marshmallows

Direction

- Set the oven to 190°C or 375°F and coat a 13"x9" casserole dish with grease.
- In a bowl, toss brown sugar and sweet potatoes together until coated well, then place in the prepared casserole dish. Put marshmallow and sweet potatoes on top.
- In the preheated oven, bake for 35 minutes until marshmallow is browned and sweet potatoes are softened.

Nutrition Information

- Calories: 270 calories;
- Total Carbohydrate: 68.3
- Cholesterol: 0
- Protein: 1.6
- Total Fat: 0.1
- Sodium: 68

91. Easy Stuffing

Serving: 8 | Prep: | Ready in:

Ingredients

- 6 ounces dry bread stuffing mix
- 10 slices day-old bread, torn into small pieces
- 3 eggs, beaten
- 1/2 cup water

Direction

- Preheat an oven to 175°C/350°F. Spray/butter one 2-qt. casserole dish.
- Follow the box directions to prep stuffing; put stuffing in a big bowl.
- Add water, eggs and dried bread; stir well, then put in casserole dish.
- Cover; bake for 45-60 minutes.

Nutrition Information

- Calories: 192 calories;
- Sodium: 577
- Total Carbohydrate: 32.2
- Cholesterol: 70
- Protein: 7.1
- Total Fat: 3.6

92. Easy Turkey Gravy

Serving: 28 | Prep: 10mins | Ready in:

Ingredients

- 5 cups turkey stock with pan drippings
- 1 (10.75 ounce) can condensed cream of chicken soup
- 1 teaspoon poultry seasoning
- 1/2 teaspoon black pepper
- 1 teaspoon seasoned salt
- 1/4 teaspoon garlic powder
- 1 cup milk
- 1/3 cup all-purpose flour

Direction

- In a big saucepan, boil turkey stock. Mix in soup, and season with garlic powder, seasoned salt, pepper, and poultry seasoning. Turn heat down to low, and allow to simmer.
- In the microwave, warm the milk, and use a fork to mix in the flour till no lumps. Bring the gravy back to a boil, and slowly mix in the milk mixture. Keep on cooking for a minute, mixing continuously, till thickened. Keep the bottom from scorching.

Nutrition Information

- Calories: 22 calories;
- Total Fat: 1
- Sodium: 227
- Total Carbohydrate: 2.5
- Cholesterol: 2
- Protein: 0.9

93. Easy Turkey Tetrazzini

Serving: 6 | Prep: 20mins | Ready in:

Ingredients

- 1 (8 ounce) package cooked egg noodles
- 2 tablespoons butter
- 1 (6 ounce) can sliced mushrooms
- 1 teaspoon salt
- 1/8 teaspoon pepper
- 2 cups chopped cooked turkey
- 1 (10.75 ounce) can condensed cream of celery soup
- 1 cup sour cream
- 1/2 cup grated Parmesan cheese

Direction

- Fill a big pot up with lightly salted water and bring it to a boil. Insert the pasta and cook until al dente, about 8-10 minutes. Drain. Preheat the oven to 375°F (190°C).
- In a big heavy skillet, melt butter and sauté the mushrooms in it for 1 minute. Sprinkle salt and pepper to season then stir in the turkey, sour cream and condensed soup. Transfer the cooked noodles into a 9x13-inch baking dish then pour the sauce mixture atop evenly. Scatter some Parmesan cheese over it. Put the dish into the preheated oven. Bake until the sauce is bubbling, about 20-25 minutes.

Nutrition Information

- Calories: 411 calories;
- Sodium: 1082
- Total Carbohydrate: 33.5
- Cholesterol: 105
- Protein: 24
- Total Fat: 20.1

94. Excellent And Healthy Cornbread

Serving: 12 | Prep: 10mins | Ready in:

Ingredients

- 1 cup unbleached flour
- 1 cup cornmeal
- 1/4 cup white sugar
- 1 teaspoon baking soda
- 3/4 teaspoon salt
- 1 cup plain nonfat yogurt
- 2 eggs, beaten

Direction

- Preheat the oven to 200°C or 400°F. Lightly oil a baking pan, 8x8-inch in size.
- Combine salt, soda, sugar, cornmeal and flour in a big bowl. Mix in eggs and yogurt. Avoid excessive mixing, mix only till well incorporated. Into prepped pan, put the batter.
- In preheated oven, allow to bake for 20 to 25 minutes, or till middle of bread springs back when touched gently.

Nutrition Information

- Calories: 76 calories;
- Total Fat: 1.2
- Sodium: 281
- Total Carbohydrate: 13.6
- Cholesterol: 31
- Protein: 3

95. Fall Apple Pumpkin Shandy

Serving: 1 | Prep: 5mins | Ready in:

Ingredients

- 6 fluid ounces pumpkin ale
- 4 fluid ounces apple cider

Direction

- In a pint glass, put in the ale then gradually mix in the apple cider.

Nutrition Information

- Calories: 145 calories;
- Total Fat: 0
- Sodium: 15
- Total Carbohydrate: 21.5
- Cholesterol: 0
- Protein: 1.1

96. Famous No Coffee Pumpkin Latte

Serving: 4 | Prep: 5mins | Ready in:

Ingredients

- 1 cup pumpkin puree
- 1 quart milk
- 1/4 cup white sugar
- 1 teaspoon ground cinnamon
- 1 tablespoon vanilla extract

Direction

- In a large saucepan, combine vanilla, cinnamon, sugar, milk and pumpkin over medium heat. Blend well with a whisk. Let heat to a simmer but don't boil.

Nutrition Information

- Calories: 202 calories;
- Total Carbohydrate: 29.7
- Cholesterol: 20
- Protein: 8.8
- Total Fat: 5
- Sodium: 248

97. French Stuffing

Serving: 6 | Prep: 5mins | Ready in:

Ingredients

- 1 pound lean ground beef
- 1 pound ground pork
- 1 onion, chopped
- 3 potatoes, peeled and diced
- 1/2 teaspoon ground cinnamon
- 1/2 teaspoon ground nutmeg
- 1 tablespoon poultry seasoning
- 1 pinch brown sugar
- 1/2 cup water
- 1 tablespoon all-purpose flour
- 1 tablespoon butter
- salt and pepper to taste

Direction

- Cook pork and beef in a large skillet over medium heat until browned. Mix in cinnamon, poultry seasoning, water, brown sugar, onion, nutmeg, and potatoes. Cover the skillet. Adjust the heat to low. Simmer the mixture for 20 minutes. Mix in pepper, salt, flour, and butter for 5-10 minutes until thickened.

Nutrition Information

- Calories: 421 calories;
- Total Fat: 23.4
- Sodium: 99
- Total Carbohydrate: 22.9
- Cholesterol: 100
- Protein: 28.7

98. Fresh Cranberry Sauce

Serving: 16 | Prep: 5mins | Ready in:

Ingredients

- 1 cup water
- 1 cup white sugar
- 1 (12 ounce) package fresh cranberries (such as Ocean Spray®)

Direction

- In a saucepan, bring water to a boil, then put in sugar and cook for 5 minutes, until sugar has dissolved. Combine sugar water and cranberries together, and then bring to a boil. Lower heat to low and simmer for 10 minutes, until the mixture reaches desired consistency.

Nutrition Information

- Calories: 58 calories;
- Total Fat: 0
- Sodium: 1
- Total Carbohydrate: 15.1
- Cholesterol: 0
- Protein: 0.1

99. Fresh Sweet Cranberry Sauce With A Twist

Serving: 6 | Prep: 5mins | Ready in:

Ingredients

- 1 1/2 cups white sugar
- 2/3 cup water
- 1 teaspoon ground cinnamon
- 1 (12 ounce) package fresh cranberries, rinsed

Direction

- In a saucepan, stir together the cinnamon, water and sugar, then bring the mixture to a boil. Put into the boiling mixture with cranberries and cook for 10 minutes, until they start to pop. Transfer the cranberry mixture into a glass bowl.
- Chill until fully chilled, while stirring from time to time.

Nutrition Information

- Calories: 220 calories;
- Total Fat: 0.1
- Sodium: 2

- Total Carbohydrate: 57.1
- Cholesterol: 0
- Protein: 0.2

100. Funky Fresh Pumpkin Pie

Serving: 8 | Prep: 10mins | Ready in:

Ingredients

- 1 pastry for a 9-inch pie crust
- 2 cups peeled chopped pumpkin
- 1 (14 ounce) can sweetened condensed milk
- 2 eggs
- 4 teaspoons light brown sugar
- 1/2 teaspoon ground nutmeg
- 1/2 teaspoon ground cinnamon
- 1/4 teaspoon ground ginger
- 1/3 cup chopped pecans

Direction

- Preheat the oven to 220°C or 425°F. Pat pie crust into a pie pan, 9-inch in size.
- In a bowl, beat eggs, sweetened condensed milk and pumpkin for about 30 seconds till smooth. Put ginger, cinnamon, nutmeg and light brown sugar; beat till equally incorporated. Into the prepped pie crust, put the mixture. Scatter pecans on top of filling.
- On a baking sheet, put the pie and cover using an aluminum foil sheet.
- In preheated oven, bake for 15 minutes. Lower temperature to 175°C or 350°F and takes off aluminum foil. Into a flattened tube-shape, roll the aluminum foil and using aluminum foil, cover the crust. Bake for half an hour. Take off aluminum foil and allow to bake for about 5 minutes longer till pie is firm in the center and crust is browned lightly.

Nutrition Information

- Calories: 338 calories;
- Total Carbohydrate: 42
- Cholesterol: 63
- Protein: 7.6
- Total Fat: 16.3
- Sodium: 198

101. Garlic Butter Acorn Squash

Serving: 4 | Prep: 5mins | Ready in:

Ingredients

- cooking spray
- 2 acorn squash, halved and seeded
- 1/4 cup butter, divided
- 4 teaspoons minced garlic, divided
- salt and ground black pepper to taste

Direction

- Set the oven to 200°C or 400°F for preheating. Use cooking spray to coat a 13"x9" baking dish.
- In the baking dish, arrange each squash half, cut side facing down.
- In the preheated oven, bake squash for a half hour, then turn squash over and put into each squash 1 tsp. of garlic as well as 1 tbsp. of butter. Use pepper and salt to season.
- Bake squash, cut-side facing up for 20 minutes longer, until softened. Allow to cool for 5 minutes before serving.

Nutrition Information

- Calories: 206 calories;
- Protein: 2.3
- Total Fat: 11.8
- Sodium: 90
- Total Carbohydrate: 27
- Cholesterol: 31

102. Garlic Mashed Cauliflower

Serving: 4 | Prep: 15mins | Ready in:

Ingredients

- 1 head cauliflower, cut into florets
- 1 tablespoon olive oil
- 1 clove garlic, smashed
- 1/4 cup grated Parmesan cheese
- 1 tablespoon reduced-fat cream cheese
- 1/2 teaspoon kosher salt
- 1/8 teaspoon freshly ground black pepper

Direction

- In a saucepan, put a steamer and fill with water to just under the base of the steamer. Boil the water. Put in cauliflower, cover, and allow it to steam for 10 minutes till tender.
- Meantime, in a small skillet, heat olive oil over medium heat; cook and mix garlic for 2 minutes till softened. Take away from heat.
- In a food processor, put 1/2 the cauliflower; put lid and blend on high. Put in the rest of cauliflower florets, one by one, till vegetables are creamy. Blend in black pepper, salt, cream cheese, Parmesan cheese and garlic.

Nutrition Information

- Calories: 98 calories;
- Total Fat: 5.7
- Sodium: 372
- Total Carbohydrate: 8.4
- Cholesterol: 7
- Protein: 5.2

103. Ginger Cinnamon Cranberry Sauce

Serving: 12 | Prep: 5mins | Ready in:

Ingredients

- 1 cup water
- 1 cup white sugar
- 2 cups fresh cranberries
- 1 (1 inch) piece fresh ginger, peeled
- 1 cinnamon stick

Direction

- Bring sugar and water in a pot to a boil on moderate heat, then boil about 5 minutes while stirring sometimes. Put in cinnamon stick, ginger and cranberries, then take the mixture back to a boil and cook for 5 minutes, until the cranberries begin popping. Turn the sauce to a shallow container, then refrigerate in the fridge for 3 hours, until chilled.

Nutrition Information

- Calories: 74 calories;
- Sodium: 1
- Total Carbohydrate: 19.2
- Cholesterol: 0
- Protein: 0.1
- Total Fat: 0

104. Give Me Seconds Oyster Dressing

Serving: 10 | Prep: 10mins | Ready in:

Ingredients

- 1 pint shelled oysters, drained
- 3/4 cup half-and-half cream
- 1/4 cup Worcestershire sauce
- 2 cups crushed buttery round crackers

- 1/2 cup butter or margarine, melted

Direction

- Preheat an oven to 175°C/350°F then grease 2-qt. baking dish.
- Mix Worcestershire sauce, half and half and oysters in medium bowl; evenly spread in prepped baking dish. Mix butter and crackers in small bowl; sprinkle over oyster mixture.
- In preheated oven, bake till dressing is hot and top is browned nicely for 30 minutes.

Nutrition Information

- Calories: 364 calories;
- Sodium: 586
- Total Carbohydrate: 29.8
- Cholesterol: 49
- Protein: 5.6
- Total Fat: 24.6

105. Glazed Carrots

Serving: 8 | Prep: 10mins | Ready in:

Ingredients

- 2 pounds carrots, peeled and cut into sticks
- 1/4 cup butter
- 1/4 cup packed brown sugar
- 1/4 teaspoon salt
- 1/8 teaspoon ground white pepper

Direction

- In a big saucepan, add carrots and enough water to fill until 1 inch deep, then bring to a boil. Lower the heat to low, then cover and simmer carrots for 8-10 minutes until softened. Drain and turn onto a bowl.
- In the same saucepan, melt butter, then stir in white pepper, salt and brown sugar until salt as well as brown sugar are dissolved. Add carrots to brown sugar sauce, then cook and stir for 5 minutes longer until carrots are glazed with sauce.

Nutrition Information

- Calories: 124 calories;
- Total Fat: 6
- Sodium: 194
- Total Carbohydrate: 17.6
- Cholesterol: 15
- Protein: 1.1

106. Glazed Carrots And Brussels Sprouts

Serving: 8 | Prep: 15mins | Ready in:

Ingredients

- 1 2/3 pounds Brussels sprouts, trimmed
- 1 pound carrots, cut into 1-inch pieces
- 2 tablespoons butter
- 2 tablespoons chopped onion
- 1 (10.5 ounce) can condensed beef consomme (such as Campbell's®)
- 1/3 cup apple juice
- 2 tablespoons cornstarch
- 2 teaspoons lemon juice
- 1 tablespoon brown sugar
- 2 pinches ground cloves, or to taste

Direction

- Pour in enough water to fill up 3/4 of a big pot. Lead it to boiling point then insert the carrots and Brussels sprouts. Lead it back to boiling point, cooking for 8 to 10 minutes until the vegetables tenderize before draining. Put butter into saucepan and warm it up at medium heat. Add onion, cooking and stirring for around 5 minutes with melted butter until the onion tenderizes. Put in the cloves, brown sugar, lemon juice, corn-starch, apple juice and beef consommé, cooking for around 5 minutes until the sauce thickens. During the process, stir regularly. Finish off by folding the carrots and Brussels sprouts in the sauce.

Nutrition Information

- Calories: 113 calories;
- Total Fat: 3.4
- Sodium: 206
- Total Carbohydrate: 19.1
- Cholesterol: 8
- Protein: 4.2

107. Gluten Free Sausage Gravy

Serving: 16 | Prep: 10mins | Ready in:

Ingredients

- 1 pound bulk pork sausage
- 1 cup unsalted butter
- 10 tablespoons gluten-free all purpose baking flour
- 1 teaspoon salt
- 60 grinds black pepper, divided
- 6 cups milk, divided
- salt to taste (optional)

Direction

- Over medium-high heat, heat a big skillet. Cook and mix sausage for 5 to 7 minutes in the hot skillet till crumbly and browned; drain and throw grease. Turn heat down to low.
- In cooked sausage, mix butter till melted; mix in flour. Cook for 5 to 10 minutes, mixing continuously, till mixture color resemble of a peanut butter. Season with 30 grinds of black pepper and a teaspoon salt.
- Raise heat to medium and add 3 cups milk. Simmer, mixing continuously. Mix in leftover 3 cups milk, a quarter cup at time, letting mixture return to a simmer after every

addition for 10 to 15 minutes. Keep cooking and mixing for 5 to 10 minutes till preferred thickness is reached. Season with salt and 30 grinds of black pepper to taste.

Nutrition Information

- Calories: 247 calories;
- Protein: 7.9
- Total Fat: 19.7
- Sodium: 449
- Total Carbohydrate: 10.8
- Cholesterol: 54

108. Graham Cracker Carmelitas

Serving: 24 | Prep: 20mins | Ready in:

Ingredients

- 12 whole graham crackers
- 1 cup margarine (such as Parkay®)
- 1 cup brown sugar
- 1 cup chopped pecans

Direction

- Set the oven to 175°C or 350°F to preheat.
- Break each graham cracker into four even pieces, make totally 48 pieces. Place closely together on a baking sheet with graham cracker pieces.
- In a heavy pan, melt margarine on moderate heat then put in brown sugar. Cook and stir the mixture until frothy and boiling. Boil about 2 minutes longer while stirring continuously. Take away from the heat and fold in pecans. Drizzle over graham crackers with caramel mixture and spread evenly.
- In the preheated oven, bake for 8-10 minutes, until caramel mixture is baked into graham crackers. Take out of the baking sheet instantly and allow cooling on an aluminum foil sheet.

Nutrition Information

- Calories: 163 calories;
- Total Fat: 11.5
- Sodium: 133
- Total Carbohydrate: 15.1
- Cholesterol: 0
- Protein: 1

109. Grand Marnier Apples With Ice Cream

Serving: 4 | Prep: 5mins | Ready in:

Ingredients

- 4 cups orange juice
- 4 apples - peeled, cored and sliced
- 4 teaspoons ground cinnamon
- 4 scoops vanilla ice cream
- 1/4 cup brandy-based orange liqueur (such as Grand Marnier®)
- 1/4 cup amaretto liqueur
- 4 chocolate wafer cookies

Direction

- In a saucepan, mix together the cinnamon, apples and orange juice over medium heat. Simmer mixture until soft, or about 5 minutes.
- Scoop the ice cream in serving dishes. Scoop apples on top of the ice cream; drizzle amaretto liqueur and Grand Marnier over. Stick a chocolate wafer to the top of ice cream for garnish.

Nutrition Information

- Calories: 366 calories;
- Total Carbohydrate: 69.6
- Cholesterol: 9
- Protein: 3.3
- Total Fat: 4

- Sodium: 58

110. Grandma's Wassail

Serving: 36 | Prep: 10mins | Ready in:

Ingredients

- 2 gallons apple cider
- 2 cups fresh orange juice
- 1 cup lemon juice
- 1 cup pineapple juice
- 1 cup white sugar
- 1 teaspoon whole cloves
- 1 cinnamon stick, broken into pieces

Direction

- On medium-low heat, combine sugar, apple cider, pineapple juice, orange juice, and lemon juice in a big pot.
- In a tea ball, put in cinnamon and cloves; place the ball in the mixture. Let it simmer for about 15 minutes until warmed through. Use a big ladle to serve cider from the pot.

Nutrition Information

- Calories: 151 calories;
- Sodium: 25
- Total Carbohydrate: 37.9
- Cholesterol: 0
- Protein: 0.2
- Total Fat: 0

111. Grandpop Joe's Challah Bread Stuffing

Serving: 8 | Prep: 15mins | Ready in:

Ingredients

- 1/2 cup unsalted butter
- 1 large onion, chopped
- 1 turkey liver, chopped
- 1 (1 pound) loaf challah bread, cut into 1-inch cubes
- salt to taste
- 2 eggs, lightly beaten

Direction

- Put butter in a skillet and heat it over medium. Mix in onion. Cook and stir for 5 minutes until the onion turned translucent and soft. Add the liver and cook while stirring for 5-7 minutes until browned all over. Remove it from the heat. Cool until just warm.
- In a large bowl, add the challah bread. Toss it with the liver and onion mixture, squeezing it lightly until the liquid is well-distributed. Whisk in beaten eggs. Season the mixture with salt.

Nutrition Information

- Calories: 323 calories;
- Protein: 9.8
- Total Fat: 18.8
- Sodium: 306
- Total Carbohydrate: 29.1
- Cholesterol: 155

112. Great Aunt D.J.'s Corn Pudding

Serving: 8 | Prep: 15mins | Ready in:

Ingredients

- 1/4 cup white sugar
- 3 tablespoons all-purpose flour
- 2 teaspoons baking powder
- 2 teaspoons salt
- 6 large eggs
- 2 cups heavy whipping cream
- 1/2 cup butter, melted
- 6 cups frozen corn

Direction

- Preheat oven to 350 °F (175 °C). Grease lightly a baking dish, 9x13-inches in size.
- In a bowl, mix together the baking powder, salt, flour, and sugar.
- In a large bowl, beat eggs together until well mixed; mix in butter and cream. Stir sugar mixture gradually into egg mixture until smooth; fold in corn until coated evenly. In the prepared baking dish, pour corn mixture.
- Bake in the preheated oven for around 45 minutes until pudding is lightly browned and set in the middle.

Nutrition Information

- Calories: 504 calories;
- Sodium: 864
- Total Carbohydrate: 36.4
- Cholesterol: 252
- Protein: 10.1
- Total Fat: 38.2

113. Green Bean Casserole

Serving: 4 | Prep: 5mins | Ready in:

Ingredients

- 1 (14.5 ounce) can French style green beans, drained
- 1 (10.75 ounce) can condensed cream of mushroom soup
- 1 (6 ounce) can French-fried onions

Direction

- Preheat the oven to 175 degrees C (350 degrees F).
- In a small casserole dish, combine the soup and green beans.

- Bake in the preheated oven for around 10-15 minutes. Remove from the oven and lay onions on top. Continue to bake for 10 minutes more and enjoy.

Nutrition Information

- Calories: 352 calories;
- Cholesterol: 0
- Protein: 2.1
- Total Fat: 25.5
- Sodium: 1187
- Total Carbohydrate: 26.6

114. Green Bean Casserole With Pumpkin Seed Crumble (Eat Clean For Thanksgiving)

Serving: 4 | Prep: 10mins | Ready in:

Ingredients

- 1 tablespoon sea salt
- 1 pound fresh green beans, trimmed
- 2 tablespoons extra-virgin olive oil, divided
- 1 tablespoon minced garlic
- 1 (8 ounce) package baby portobello mushrooms, stemmed and roughly chopped
- salt to taste
- 1/2 teaspoon ground white pepper, or to taste, divided
- 2 tablespoons white whole wheat flour (such as King Arthur®)
- 2 tablespoons whole milk (such as Natural by Nature®)
- 1/2 cup pumpkin seeds
- 1/4 cup whole wheat panko bread crumbs
- 2 teaspoons extra-virgin olive oil

Direction

- Set oven to 425°F (220°C) to preheat. Lightly oil a 9x13-inch glass baking pan.
- In a large bowl, place ice and pour in cold water to make an ice bath.
- Bring a large pot of water and 1 tablespoon salt to a boil. Add green beans; boil for 5 to 6 minutes until beans are fork-tender. Transfer beans to a colander to drain, and then immerse them right away into the ice bath. Drain one more time. Transfer to paper towels or a kitchen towel to pat dry.
- In a large skillet, heat 1 tablespoon oil over medium-high heat. Sauté garlic in heated oil for 1 minute; stir in mushrooms; sauté for about 5 minutes until tender. Sprinkle with white pepper and salt to taste. Turn off the heat. Mix in the cooked green beans and toss. Pour the bean mixture into the prepared baking pan. Heat 1 tablespoon oil and flour over medium-high heat in the skillet; cook for about 1 minute, stirring frequently, until well distributed. Gradually pour in milk, stirring for about 2 minutes, until the roux becomes creamy and smooth. Sprinkle with white pepper and salt to taste. Mix roux into the pan, tossing gently until the green bean-mushroom mixture is evenly coated.
- Place 2 teaspoons oil, bread crumbs, and pumpkin seeds together into a food processor. Pulse about 10 times until it becomes ground. Add salt to season; pulse one more time. Pour processed pumpkin seed mixture over the top of green bean-mushroom mixture.
- Bake for about 10 minutes in the preheated oven until surface turns golden brown.

Nutrition Information

- Calories: 261 calories;
- Protein: 9
- Total Fat: 17.7
- Sodium: 1383
- Total Carbohydrate: 21
- Cholesterol: 1

115. Green Bean And Potato Casserole

Serving: 6 | Prep: 15mins | Ready in:

Ingredients

- 2 (14 ounce) cans green beans, drained
- 2 (15 ounce) cans diced potatoes, drained
- 1 (10.75 ounce) can condensed cream of chicken soup
- 1 pound shredded Colby cheese

Direction

- Turn oven to 350°F (175°C) to preheat. Lightly oil a small casserole dish. In the prepared casserole dish, combine cheese, cream of chicken soup, potatoes, and green beans. Bake, covered in the preheated oven for half an hour. Uncover, and keep baking until casserole is lightly browned and bubbly, or for 15 minutes.

Nutrition Information

- Calories: 450 calories;
- Total Carbohydrate: 29
- Cholesterol: 76
- Protein: 22.3
- Total Fat: 27.5
- Sodium: 1467

116. Grilled Turkey Breast With Fresh Sage Leaves

Serving: 8 | Prep: 20mins | Ready in:

Ingredients

- 3 tablespoons freshly squeezed lemon juice
- 3 tablespoons extra-virgin olive oil
- 28 leaves fresh sage
- 4 skinless, boneless turkey breast halves
- sea salt and freshly ground black pepper to taste
- 2 tablespoons extra-virgin olive oil
- 3 tablespoons unsalted butter
- 2 lemons, halved

Direction

- Combine 3 tablespoons olive oil, sage leaves, and lemon juice in a big container, mix them together and put the turkey breast halves into the mixture. Marinate the breasts at room temperature for 30 minutes and occasionally turn over the meat.
- Prepare the grill by preheating it to medium heat then coat the grate lightly with oil.
- Take the turkey breasts out of the marinade and set the marinade and sage leaves aside.
- Dash with sea salt and black pepper on both sides of the turkey.
- Cook the turkey breasts on the grill for about 30 minutes until grill marks appear, the inside of the meat is no longer pink and an instant-read meat thermometer reads at least 160° F (70° C) when inserted into the thickest part of the turkey breast. Flip over the turkey pieces after 15 minutes.
- Heat 2 tablespoons olive oil mixed with unsalted butter in a large pan on medium high-heat until hot and bubbles form, while the turkey is grilling. Add the marinate and the sage that you've set aside, into the oil and butter and continue cooking and stirring for 10 to 15 minutes until the marinade completely evaporates and the sage leaves are fried to crispiness.
- Move the grilled meat to a cutting board and add salt and black pepper, seasoning if you prefer; cut the turkey in diagonal thick slices and arrange the slices on a plate. Top the turkey slices with fried sage leaves and put lemon halves for garnish.

Nutrition Information

- Calories: 377 calories;
- Total Carbohydrate: 3.8

- Cholesterol: 168
- Protein: 57.1
- Total Fat: 14.3
- Sodium: 139

117. Holiday Cranberry Punch

Serving: 7 | Prep: 10mins | Ready in:

Ingredients

- 1 (16 ounce) can jellied cranberry sauce
- 3/4 cup orange juice
- 1/4 cup lemon juice
- 2 cups ice, or as needed
- 3 1/2 cups chilled ginger ale

Direction

- In a blender, process cranberry sauce until smooth. Put in lemon juice and orange juice then blend more until smooth.
- In a pitcher, mix ice and cranberry mixture. Pour the ginger ale into cranberry mixture gradually and stir gently to mix.

Nutrition Information

- Calories: 154 calories;
- Total Fat: 0.1
- Sodium: 36
- Total Carbohydrate: 39.1
- Cholesterol: 0
- Protein: 0.3

118. Holiday Ginger Snap Crust

Serving: 8 | Prep: 10mins | Ready in:

Ingredients

- 1 1/2 cups crushed gingersnap cookies
- 1/3 cup brown sugar
- 6 tablespoons melted butter
- 12 gingersnap cookies, or as needed

Direction

- Start preheating the oven to 375°F (190°C).
- In a bowl, mix together butter, brown sugar and crushed gingersnap cookies until combined well. Press gingersnap mixture into a springform pan bottom. Place all gingersnap cookies upright around the springform pan border, pressing them into base to stand firmly.
- Bake in prepared oven for set 7 mins or until. Let cool completely.

Nutrition Information

- Calories: 257 calories;
- Total Carbohydrate: 32.1
- Cholesterol: 23
- Protein: 1.4
- Total Fat: 14
- Sodium: 182

119. Homemade Cranberry Ginger Sauce

Serving: 12 | Prep: 15mins | Ready in:

Ingredients

- 2 oranges, zested and juiced
- 1/2 cup honey, or more to taste
- 2 pieces of crystallized ginger, chopped - or more to taste
- 1 cinnamon stick
- 1/4 teaspoon salt
- 1 (12 ounce) package fresh cranberries

Direction

- In a saucepan, combine salt, cinnamon stick, crystallized ginger, honey, orange juice, and orange zest over medium heat; simmer. Mix cranberries into the orange juice mixture, put a cover on and boil for 1 minute. Lower the heat to low. Simmer the cranberry sauce for 15 minutes until the cranberries burst. Take away from heat and remove the cinnamon stick. If you want the sauce to be sweeter, mix in extra honey. Enjoy chilled or warm.

Nutrition Information

- Calories: 57 calories;
- Total Fat: 0
- Sodium: 50
- Total Carbohydrate: 15.5
- Cholesterol: 0
- Protein: 0.2

120. Homemade Turkey Gravy

Serving: 16 | Prep: 10mins | Ready in:

Ingredients

- 2 cups turkey drippings, or as needed
- 1/4 cup all-purpose flour
- 1 cup chicken broth, or more as needed
- salt and ground black pepper to taste

Direction

- Pour the drippings into a clear 4-cup measuring cup, to part the oil from the liquid in the turkey drippings. Let drippings to settle and separate into juices on the bottom and oil on top. Use a kitchen syringe to remove a quarter cup of oil; move to a saucepan.
- In the saucepan, stir flour into the oil; cook and mix for 5 minutes over medium-low heat till color turns to a light brown. In flour mixture, put 1 cup juices from the measuring cup to create roux; cook and mix for 5 minutes, putting in extra drippings to thin gravy, till gravy is smooth and heated through. Stir chicken broth into gravy; cook and mix for 5 minutes till heated through, putting in extra broth to thin gravy.

Nutrition Information

- Calories: 239 calories;
- Total Fat: 25.6
- Sodium: 70
- Total Carbohydrate: 1.6
- Cholesterol: 26
- Protein: 0.3

121. Homesteader Cornbread

Serving: 15 | Prep: 15mins | Ready in:

Ingredients

- 1 1/2 cups cornmeal
- 2 1/2 cups milk
- 2 cups all-purpose flour
- 1 tablespoon baking powder
- 1 teaspoon salt
- 2/3 cup white sugar
- 2 eggs
- 1/2 cup vegetable oil

Direction

- Preheat the oven to 200 °C or 400 °F. Mix milk and cornmeal in a small bowl; let sit for 5 minutes. Oil a baking pan, 9x13 inch in size.
- Beat together sugar, salt, baking powder and flour in a big bowl. Stir in oil, eggs and cornmeal mixture till smooth. Put batter into the prepared pan.
- In the prepared oven, bake for 30 to 35 minutes till a knife inserted into the middle of cornbread comes out clean.

Nutrition Information

- Calories: 234 calories;
- Sodium: 253
- Total Carbohydrate: 33.1
- Cholesterol: 28
- Protein: 4.9
- Total Fat: 9.3

122. Honey Glazed Carrots And Pears

Serving: 12 | Prep: 15mins | Ready in:

Ingredients

- 3 Anjou pears, peeled and cut into chunks
- 3 pounds carrots, peeled and sliced
- 1 cup butter
- 2 tablespoons brown sugar
- 2 tablespoons honey
- 1 teaspoon ground cinnamon
- 1/2 teaspoon ground nutmeg
- 1 tablespoon chopped fresh parsley, or as needed

Direction

- Set the steamer insert into the saucepan filled with water, just below the steamers' bottom. Bring the water to a boil. Add pears and cover the pan. Let them steam for 5-10 minutes until tender. Place the pears into a bowl. Add carrots to the steamer and cover the pan. Cook for 10 minutes until tender. Place the carrots into the bowl with pears.
- Put butter in a saucepan and heat it over medium. Mix in the cinnamon, honey, nutmeg, and brown sugar. Bring the mixture to a simmer for 5-10 minutes, stirring occasionally until the glaze is reduced slightly and the sugar has melted.
- Drizzle carrots and pears with glaze, tossing them until coated. Use a slotted spoon to transfer the carrots and pears into the serving dish. Sprinkle them with parsley.

Nutrition Information

- Calories: 227 calories;
- Sodium: 189
- Total Carbohydrate: 22.6
- Cholesterol: 41
- Protein: 1.4
- Total Fat: 15.7

123. Hot Mulled Wine

Serving: 9 | Prep: 5mins | Ready in:

Ingredients

- 1 1/2 cups boiling water
- 1/2 cup white sugar
- 1/4 lemon
- 8 whole cloves
- 1 (3 inch) cinnamon stick
- 1 (750 milliliter) bottle claret wine
- 1 pinch ground nutmeg (optional)

Direction

- In a saucepan, stir sugar and water together till sugar is dissolved. Add cinnamon sticks, cloves and lemon. Boil and cook for 10 minutes to combine the flavors. Strain and bring the water mixture back to the saucepan. Remove cinnamon stick, cloves and lemon.
- Add claret wine in the water mixture and stir. Heat for 5-10 minutes till hot, don't boil. Serve the drink flecked along with nutmeg.

Nutrition Information

- Calories: 106 calories;
- Sodium: 10
- Total Carbohydrate: 13.5
- Cholesterol: 0
- Protein: 0.3
- Total Fat: 0.1

124. Incredible Red Smashed Potatoes

Serving: 8 | Prep: 15mins | Ready in:

Ingredients

- 3 pounds red potatoes
- 1 tablespoon kosher salt
- 1 1/2 cups half-and-half
- 1/2 cup butter
- 1/2 cup sour cream
- 2 teaspoons kosher salt
- 1 teaspoon ground black pepper

Direction

- In a large pot, put potatoes and 1 tablespoon kosher salt, fill water to cover; bring to a boil. Then lower the heat to medium-low; simmer, covered, for 25-35 minutes until soft. Let drain and transfer the potatoes to a large bowl.
- In a small saucepan, mix butter and half-and-half over medium-low heat for 5-10 minutes, or until heated through and the butter is melted.
- In the large bowl, blend the potatoes using an electric hand mixer until mashed. Pour 3/4 the cream-butter mixture slowly into the blended potatoes; then mix on the lowest speed until completely combined. Next, fold in the sour cream and the remaining 1/4 cream-butter mixture. Season with black pepper and 2 teaspoons kosher salt.

Nutrition Information

- Calories: 311 calories;
- Total Fat: 20
- Sodium: 1318
- Total Carbohydrate: 29.8
- Cholesterol: 54
- Protein: 5.2

125. Insanely Easy Cranberry Sauce

Serving: 8 | Prep: 10mins | Ready in:

Ingredients

- 2 1/2 cups white wine
- 2 cups white sugar
- 2 tablespoons ground cinnamon
- 1 pinch ground ginger
- 3/4 pound fresh cranberries
- 1/4 pound fresh cherries, pitted and halved

Direction

- On medium-high heat, simmer ginger, wine, cinnamon, and sugar together in a pot; mix until the sugar dissolves. Put in cherries and cranberries; continue simmering on medium-low heat for 45mins, covered, while mixing from time to time. Place in the refrigerator until ready to serve.

Nutrition Information

- Calories: 292 calories;
- Protein: 0.5
- Total Fat: 0.2
- Sodium: 5
- Total Carbohydrate: 61
- Cholesterol: 0

126. Instant Pot® Thanksgiving Dinner

Serving: 4 | Prep: 25mins | Ready in:

Ingredients

- 4 sweet potatoes
- 2 tablespoons maple syrup
- salt to taste

- 1 turkey breast
- 2 tablespoons barbeque dry rub (such as Charlie Vergos Rendezvous Famous Seasoning®)
- 1/2 cup butter, divided
- 1 cup chopped celery
- 1 small onion, chopped
- 3 cups crumbled cornbread
- 1/2 cup chopped pecans
- 2 slices crisp cooked bacon, cut into 1/2-inch pieces
- 1/2 teaspoon barbeque dry rub (such as Charlie Vergos Rendezvous Famous Seasoning®)
- 1 1/2 cups turkey stock

Direction

- Poke holes in a sweet potato using a fork; microwave for 8-10 minutes until tender on high. Set aside for 10 minutes until cool enough to hold; peel and mash in a bowl. Add maple syrup and salt then mix.
- Switch on an electric pressure cooker, like Instant Pot®, and place on "Sauté" mode. Rub barbeque seasoning on the turkey breast. Melt quarter cup butter in the cooker for 2 minutes then place in the turkey breast with the skin side down. Cook for 5 minutes until brown. Take off heat.
- On medium heat, melt the leftover quarter cup butter in a pan. Sauté onion and celery for 2 minutes until slightly soft; mix in bacon, pecans, and cornbread. Take off heat, add half teaspoon barbeque rub; mix gently.
- Make two rafts from sheets of aluminum foil. Punch holes in the first raft then fill it with cornbread mixture; place the mashed sweet potatoes in the second raft.
- Turn the turkey breast so its skin side is now up, put the raft with the cornbread mixture on top. Slowly pour stock on the dressing, the drips will make the turkey stay moist. Set the sweet potatoes raft on the dressing.
- Cover the pressure cooker, seal, and set it on the "Poultry" setting for half hour.
- Let the pressure escape naturally as specified in the manufacturer's instructions. Put aside for 5 minutes before cutting. Serve with the sweet potatoes and cornbread dressing.

Nutrition Information

- Calories: 770 calories;
- Protein: 40.2
- Total Fat: 40.3
- Sodium: 2706
- Total Carbohydrate: 62.7
- Cholesterol: 173

127. Instant Pot® Turkey Breast

Serving: 8 | Prep: 10mins | Ready in:

Ingredients

- 1 (1 ounce) package onion soup mix
- 1 (6 pound) turkey breast, thawed
- 2 ribs celery, cut into large chunks
- 1 onion, cut into large chunks
- 1 cup chicken broth
- 2 tablespoons water
- 1 tablespoon cornstarch, or more as needed

Direction

- Rub onion soup mix all over turkey breast. Put turkey breast in the electric pressure cooker pot (like Instant Pot®). Add onion chunks and celery on top and around turkey breast then pour chicken broth all over it.
- Close and lock pressure cooker then select Poultry in the setting to bring to high/low according to manufacturer's directions. Cook for 30 minutes until juices run clear. Using the natural-release method, carefully release pressure for about 20 minutes. Place turkey breast to a serving platter and slice.

- Adjust electric pressure cooker setting to Sauté. Mix cornstarch in a bowl of water then add a bit of hot liquid from the pot. Mix well until cornstarch dissolves then pour mixture into the pot and blend well for about 3 minutes until thickened. Serve turkey along with this prepared gravy.

Nutrition Information

- Calories: 583 calories;
- Total Fat: 22.1
- Sodium: 630
- Total Carbohydrate: 5
- Cholesterol: 220
- Protein: 85.7

128. Instant Pot® Warm Vegetarian Farro Salad With Cauliflower, Pistachios And Cranberries

Serving: 4 | Prep: 15mins | Ready in:

Ingredients

- 2 cups cauliflower florets
- 3 tablespoons olive oil, divided
- 1 1/2 teaspoons salt, divided
- 1/4 teaspoon ground black pepper
- 1/3 cup white wine
- 1/3 cup dried cranberries
- 1 tablespoon honey
- 1 1/2 cups farro
- 3 cups water
- Dressing:
- 2 teaspoons lemon juice
- 1/4 cup olive oil
- 1/2 teaspoon salt
- 1/2 teaspoon garlic powder
- 1/4 teaspoon ground black pepper
- 2 tablespoons chopped pistachio nuts

Direction

- In a mixing bowl, spice the cauliflower with 1/2 tsp. of salt, 1/4 tsp. of pepper, and 2 tbsp. of olive oil.
- In a heat-proof bowl, mix the dried cranberries, honey, and white wine together and seal it with foil.
- Press the Sauté button on multi-functional pressure cooker (such as Instant Pot®) and warm 1 tbsp. of oil. Mix in farro and 1 tsp. of salt and let it cook for 3 minutes or until shiny.
- Add water over the farro and put the steamer rack on the top. In steamer rack, arrange the bowl of cranberries mixture and the cauliflower florets. Lock the lid properly. Follow the manufacturer's instructions on how to select the high pressure setting. Set the timer for 8 mins. Allot time for the pressure to build, about 10-15 minutes.
- Allow the pressure to release following manufacturer's directions for natural-release method, 10-40 minutes. Unlock and take lid off; take bowl of cranberries, farro and cauliflower out. Strain the farro.
- For dressing, combine 1/4 tsp. of pepper, garlic, 1/2 tsp. of salt, 1 tbsp. cooking juice from cranberries, 1/4 cup of olive oil, and lemon juice together in a mixing bowl.
- Cut the cauliflower in bite-sized chunks and pour over farro in a bowl. Mix in pistachios and cranberries and top it generously with the dressing.

Nutrition Information

- Calories: 533 calories;
- Cholesterol: 0
- Protein: 9.6
- Total Fat: 27.4
- Sodium: 1204
- Total Carbohydrate: 68.3

129. Jan's Cranberry Curd

Serving: 24 | Prep: 10mins | Ready in:

Ingredients

- 2 cups fresh cranberries
- 1/2 cup water
- 3 egg yolks
- 1 large egg
- 3/4 cup white sugar
- 1/4 cup unsalted butter, diced

Direction

- Cook water and cranberries in a saucepan on medium heat for 10 minutes till cranberries start to pop and open, occasionally mixing. Use a potato masher/spoon to crush cranberries lightly; take off from the heat.
- Mix egg and egg yolks in a bowl then add sugar; whisk till smooth and frothy. Put 1 tbsp. hot cranberry mixture into the egg mixture; immediately whisk. Keep adding, 1 tbsp. at a time, hot cranberry mixture, whisking after every addition, till you incorporate 1/2 cup of hot cranberry mixture.
- Put egg-cranberry mixture into the hot cranberry mixture; whisk together immediately. Use an immersion blender to blend the mixture till curd is smooth and silky.
- Cook curd on medium heat for 5 minutes till curd coats back of the spoon and on a low boil, constantly whisking. Take the saucepan off from the heat. Put butter in curd; continuously whisk till incorporated.

Nutrition Information

- Calories: 55 calories;
- Sodium: 5
- Total Carbohydrate: 7.5
- Cholesterol: 38
- Protein: 0.6
- Total Fat: 2.7

130. Kale With Pine Nuts And Shredded Parmesan

Serving: 6 | Prep: 10mins | Ready in:

Ingredients

- 1/4 cup pine nuts
- 1/4 cup butter
- 1 bunch kale - stems removed, roughly chopped, and rinsed
- 1 teaspoon distilled white vinegar
- salt and ground black pepper to taste
- 1/2 cup shredded Parmesan cheese

Direction

- In a skillet, toast pine nuts on low heat for 5 minutes till fragrant and golden brown.
- Melt butter on medium heat in a big skillet. Put kale in melted butter; cook for 10 minutes till tender.
- Toss vinegar and cooked kale in a serving bowl; use pepper and salt to season. Sprinkle parmesan cheese. Serve.

Nutrition Information

- Calories: 166 calories;
- Total Fat: 13
- Sodium: 189
- Total Carbohydrate: 8.6
- Cholesterol: 26
- Protein: 6.5

131. Leftover Thanksgiving Wedge Pies

Serving: 4 | Prep: 15mins | Ready in:

Ingredients

- 1 (15 ounce) package pastry for a 9-inch double-crust pie
- 1/2 cup prepared mashed potatoes
- 1/2 cup shredded cooked turkey meat
- 1/4 cup cranberry sauce
- 1 egg
- 1 tablespoon water

Direction

- Start preheating the oven to 230°C (450°F). Line the parchment paper onto a baking sheet.
- On a lightly floured work surface, roll out each pastry and cut each into quarters.
- Spread about 2 tbsp. of mashed potatoes onto 4 of the pastry quarters, leave about 1/3 inch of the edges. Add 1 tbsp. of cranberry sauce and 2 tbsp. of turkey on top of mashed potatoes.
- In a bowl, stir the water and egg together. Use a brush to spread the egg mixture onto the outside edges of prepared pastry quarters. Add the remaining pastry quarters on top of each of the prepared quarter; use a fork to press and crimp the edges to seal. Slice a slit on top of each pastry wedge and brush the egg mixture onto it. Place the pies on the prepared baking dish.
- Bake for about 15-20 minutes in the preheated oven until the pies become golden brown.

Nutrition Information

- Calories: 587 calories;
- Cholesterol: 60
- Protein: 13.2
- Total Fat: 34.6
- Sodium: 619
- Total Carbohydrate: 55.6

132. Lemon Pepper Green Beans

Serving: 6 | Prep: 5mins | Ready in:

Ingredients

- 1 pound fresh green beans, rinsed and trimmed
- 2 tablespoons butter
- 1/4 cup sliced almonds
- 2 teaspoons lemon pepper

Direction

- In a steamer, put the green beans then set on top of 1-in boiling water; cover. Cook for 10 minutes until tender yet still firm; drain.
- In the meantime, melt butter on medium heat in a frying pan. Sauté almonds in melted butter until pale brown; sprinkle lemon pepper to season. Toss in green beans to coat.

Nutrition Information

- Calories: 81 calories;
- Total Fat: 5.9
- Sodium: 186
- Total Carbohydrate: 6.3
- Cholesterol: 10
- Protein: 2.3

133. Lemon Glazed Carrots

Serving: 2 | Prep: 10mins | Ready in:

Ingredients

- 2 carrots, sliced 1/4-inch thick
- 1 tablespoon butter
- 1 tablespoon brown sugar
- 1 teaspoon lemon juice
- salt and ground black pepper to taste (optional)

Direction

- In a big pot, place carrots and water to cover, then bring water to a boil. Lower heat to

medium-low and simmer for 8 minutes, until carrots are soft. Drain.
- In a skillet, heat butter on medium heat, then cook and stir together in the melted butter the lemon juice, brown sugar and carrots for 2 minutes, while stirring frequently, until sugar is dissolved.

Nutrition Information

- Calories: 102 calories;
- Total Carbohydrate: 12.7
- Cholesterol: 15
- Protein: 0.6
- Total Fat: 5.9
- Sodium: 85

134. Maple Buttercream Frosting

Serving: 24 | Prep: 15mins | Ready in:

Ingredients

- 4 cups confectioners' sugar
- 1/2 cup butter, softened
- 7 tablespoons pure maple syrup
- 3 tablespoons heavy whipping cream

Direction

- In a bowl, beat syrup, butter and confectioners' sugar with an electric mixer till smooth. Include in cream, 1 tablespoon per time; beat till the frosting becomes thick and attains the desired consistency.

Nutrition Information

- Calories: 137 calories;
- Sodium: 29
- Total Carbohydrate: 24.8
- Cholesterol: 13
- Protein: 0.1

- Total Fat: 4.6

135. Maple Cinnamon Ham Glaze

Serving: 20 | Prep: 10mins | Ready in:

Ingredients

- 1/4 cup packed dark brown sugar
- 2 teaspoons ground cinnamon
- 1 cup maple syrup

Direction

- In a bowl, stir together cinnamon and brown sugar until well mixed. Add in maple syrup and stir until smooth.

Nutrition Information

- Calories: 52 calories;
- Total Fat: 0
- Sodium: 2
- Total Carbohydrate: 13.4
- Cholesterol: 0
- Protein: 0

136. Maple Ginger Cranberry Sauce

Serving: 8 | Prep: 5mins | Ready in:

Ingredients

- 1 cup apple cider
- 1 (12 ounce) package fresh cranberries
- 1/2 cup orange juice
- 1/3 cup maple syrup
- 1 tablespoon minced fresh ginger
- 1/4 teaspoon ground allspice
- 1/4 teaspoon ground cinnamon

Direction

- In a saucepan, cook apple cider over medium-low heat for about 10 minutes until the amount of cider is decreased by half, remember to stir while cooking.
- In a saucepan, combine cinnamon, allspice, ginger, maple syrup, orange juice, cranberries and reduced apple cider; bring to a boil. Lower the heat to medium-low and simmer for about 10 minutes until the sauce is thickened and cranberries burst, remember to stir occasionally while cooking.

Nutrition Information

- Calories: 79 calories;
- Sodium: 6
- Total Carbohydrate: 20
- Cholesterol: 0
- Protein: 0.3
- Total Fat: 0.1

137. Maple Glazed Butternut Squash

Serving: 4 | Prep: 10mins | Ready in:

Ingredients

- 1 butternut squash - peeled, seeded, quartered, and cut into 1/2-inch slices
- 2/3 cup water
- 1/4 cup maple syrup
- 1/4 cup dark rum
- 1/4 teaspoon ground nutmeg

Direction

- Boil nutmeg, butternut squash, rum, maple syrup, and water together in a pot. Lower heat; let it simmer for 15mins while stirring occasionally until the squash is tender.
- With a slotted spoon move the butternut squash to a serving dish; save the liquid in the pot. Simmer for 5-10mins until the liquid is thick and reduced; pour all over the butternut squash.

Nutrition Information

- Calories: 201 calories;
- Protein: 2.6
- Total Fat: 0.4
- Sodium: 13
- Total Carbohydrate: 43.2
- Cholesterol: 0

138. Maple Glazed Carrots

Serving: 8 | Prep: 10mins | Ready in:

Ingredients

- 1 1/2 pounds baby carrots
- 1/4 cup butter
- 1/3 cup maple syrup
- salt and ground black pepper to taste

Direction

- In a pot, add carrots and salted water to cover, then bring to a boil. Lower heat to moderately low and simmer for 15-20 minutes, until soft. Drain and turn carrots to a serving bowl.
- In a saucepan, melt butter on moderately low heat. Stir into melted butter with maple syrup and cook for 1-2 minutes longer, until warmed. Drizzle over carrots with butter-maple syrup and toss to coat well. Use pepper and salt to season.

Nutrition Information

- Calories: 120 calories;
- Total Fat: 6
- Sodium: 101
- Total Carbohydrate: 17
- Cholesterol: 15

- Protein: 0.9

139. Maple Glazed Turkey Roast

Serving: 6 | Prep: 10mins | Ready in:

Ingredients

- 1 (3 pound) boneless turkey breast roast, thawed
- 1/2 cup pure maple syrup, or more as needed
- 1 teaspoon liquid smoke flavoring (optional)
- 1 teaspoon ground paprika
- 1/2 teaspoon salt
- 1/2 teaspoon pepper
- 1/2 teaspoon garlic powder
- 1/2 teaspoon onion powder
- 1/2 teaspoon dried crushed thyme
- 1 pinch cayenne pepper, or to taste

Direction

- Start preheating oven to 325°F (165°C).
- Discard plastic wrap and netting from turkey roast, if any, but retain on string netting. (Discard and remove any the gravy packet). Rinse turkey, using paper towels to pat dry.
- In a bowl, mix cayenne pepper, thyme, onion powder, garlic powder, pepper, salt, paprika, smoke flavoring and maple syrup together, stirring to combine well. Brush all over turkey roast with syrup mixture.
- In a roasting pan, put roast on a baking rack, the skin side facing up. Roast in prepared oven, until the meat thermometer registers 170°F (75°C) when inserted into middle of roast and the roast turns golden brown, basting occasionally. Roasting time is approximately 90 mins. Cover the roast with foil. Allow to stand 10 mins. Then remove string netting for slicing.

Nutrition Information

- Calories: 351 calories;
- Total Carbohydrate: 32.9
- Cholesterol: 120
- Protein: 40.1
- Total Fat: 5.9
- Sodium: 1734

140. Maple Dijon Brussels Leaf Salad

Serving: 12 | Prep: 30mins | Ready in:

Ingredients

- 2 pounds Brussels sprouts, trimmed
- 1/4 cup maple syrup
- 2 tablespoons extra-virgin olive oil
- 4 teaspoons Dijon mustard
- 4 teaspoons apple cider vinegar
- 1 cup sweetened dried cranberries
- 1 cup cinnamon-roasted almonds

Direction

- Use a paring knife to remove cores from Brussels sprouts. Detach the leaves by peeling layers apart then put them into a big bowl. In a small bowl, beat together apple cider vinegar, Dijon mustard, olive oil and maple syrup. Empty this mixture out into the big bowl with leaves. Insert cranberries. Coat everything by tossing. Insert almonds. Finish off by tossing once more when ready to serve. If not serving right away, the salad can keep in the fridge for up to 3 days.

Nutrition Information

- Calories: 173 calories;
- Total Carbohydrate: 22.1
- Cholesterol: 0
- Protein: 5.1
- Total Fat: 8.6
- Sodium: 61

141. Mashed Sweet Potatoes By Jean Carper

Serving: 6 | Prep: | Ready in:

Ingredients

- 2 1/2 pounds sweet potatoes
- 3 tablespoons Amaretto (almond liqueur) or maple syrup
- Cinnamon, to taste
- Ginger, to taste
- 1/4 cup toasted almonds

Direction

- Microwave whole potatoes until fully cooked. Let it cool to touch. Take out the pulp. Mash potatoes in liqueur and spices. Add almonds on top. Reheat in the microwave.

Nutrition Information

- Calories: 235 calories;
- Total Fat: 3.3
- Sodium: 69
- Total Carbohydrate: 44.3
- Cholesterol: 0
- Protein: 5.1

142. Mexican Turkey

Serving: 4 | Prep: 10mins | Ready in:

Ingredients

- 1 teaspoon vegetable oil
- 1 onion, chopped
- 1 pound shredded cooked turkey
- 1 teaspoon garlic powder
- 1 large fresh tomato, chopped
- 1/2 cup water
- 1 tablespoon chopped fresh cilantro
- salt and pepper to taste

Direction

- In a skillet, heat oil over moderate heat, and cook onion till soft. Stir in turkey, and put in garlic powder to season. Mix in tomato. Add water, scatter cilantro on top, and add pepper and salt to season. Place cover on skillet, and let simmer for 5 minutes, or till heated completely.

Nutrition Information

- Calories: 225 calories;
- Total Carbohydrate: 4.9
- Cholesterol: 86
- Protein: 34.1
- Total Fat: 6.9
- Sodium: 83

143. Mini Pecan Pie

Serving: 24 | Prep: 15mins | Ready in:

Ingredients

- 1/2 (8 ounce) package cream cheese, softened
- 1/2 cup margarine, softened
- 1 cup self-rising flour
- 3/4 cup packed brown sugar
- 1 egg
- 1 tablespoon ground cinnamon
- 1 teaspoon vanilla extract
- 3/4 cup chopped pecans
- 3 (1 ounce) squares semi-sweet baking chocolate

Direction

- In a bowl, with an electric mixer, beating together margarine and cream cheese till creamy and smooth. Adding flour slowly and

mixing continually till dough is smooth. Let mixture sit for 15 minutes in the refrigerator.
- In a bowl, beating together vanilla extract, cinnamon, egg and brown sugar till smooth; adding pecans and stirring.
- Heat oven to 175°C (350°F) beforehand. Greasing 24 mini muffin cups.
- In each muffin cup, spooning dough, approximately a tablespoon per pie. In every cup, pressing dough up the sides and into the bottom, making a pie shell. Use pecan mixture to fill every shell.
- In the preheated oven, allow to bake for approximately 30 minutes till pies are set. On waxed paper, place pies and let them cool down.
- In a small saucepan, melting chocolate over low heat, constantly stirring. Dipping a fork into melted chocolate and drizzling over pies.

Nutrition Information

- Calories: 139 calories;
- Total Fat: 9.2
- Sodium: 129
- Total Carbohydrate: 13.5
- Cholesterol: 13
- Protein: 1.8

144. Mini Southern Pecan Pies

Serving: 18 | Prep: 20mins | Ready in:

Ingredients

- 1 1/2 cups pecan halves
- 1 cup white sugar
- 3 eggs, beaten
- 1/2 cup light corn syrup
- 1/2 cup dark corn syrup
- 2 tablespoons butter, melted
- 1 teaspoon vanilla extract
- 1/4 teaspoon salt
- 18 (3 inch) ready-to-bake pie shells

Direction

- Set oven to 350°F (175°C), and start preheating.
- On a food processor, add pecans and pulse until chopped coarsely.
- In a bowl, combine salt, vanilla extract, butter, dark corn syrup, light corn syrup, eggs and sugar together; fold in the pecans. In each pie shell, spoon 1/4 cup of pecan mixture. On a baking sheet, arrange pies.
- Bake in the prepped oven for 25 - 30 minutes, till slightly browned.

Nutrition Information

- Calories: 319 calories;
- Total Fat: 15.1
- Sodium: 163
- Total Carbohydrate: 45.3
- Cholesterol: 35
- Protein: 3.3

145. Moe's Fabulous Mashed Potatoes

Serving: 4 | Prep: 18mins | Ready in:

Ingredients

- 1 pound Yukon Gold potatoes, peeled and quartered
- 1/2 cup whole milk
- 1/4 cup butter, cut into pieces
- 1 pinch ground nutmeg
- kosher salt to taste
- ground white pepper to taste

Direction

- In a big pot, add potatoes and salted water to cover, then bring to a boil on high heat. Lower heat to moderately low, place a cover and simmer potatoes for 20 minutes, until soften.

- Drain and let steam dry for 1-2 minutes, then remove potatoes to a big bowl.
- In a small saucepan, bring the milk to a boil on moderately low heat.
- Use an electric mixer to whip potatoes until smooth, then add boiling milk on potatoes and put in white pepper, salt, nutmeg and butter. Whip the mixture on medium speed until fluffy and light.

Nutrition Information

- Calories: 212 calories;
- Sodium: 201
- Total Carbohydrate: 22.1
- Cholesterol: 34
- Protein: 3.5
- Total Fat: 12.7

146. Mom's Barbeque Style Turkey

Serving: 6 | Prep: 10mins | Ready in:

Ingredients

- 1/4 cup butter
- 1/2 cup chopped onion
- 1 cup chopped celery
- 1/2 cup chopped green bell pepper
- 1 cup ketchup
- 3 tablespoons brown sugar
- 1 1/2 teaspoons chili powder
- 1 tablespoon Worcestershire sauce
- salt to taste
- 4 cups chopped cooked turkey

Direction

- In a skillet, liquify butter over moderate heat. In the skillet, put the green pepper, celery and onion, and allow to cook for 5 minutes. Stir in Worcestershire sauce, chili powder, brown sugar and ketchup. Add salt to season. Allow to cook over low heat till bubbly. Mix in turkey, place cover on, and simmer for half an hour.

Nutrition Information

- Calories: 307 calories;
- Cholesterol: 91
- Protein: 28.6
- Total Fat: 12.6
- Sodium: 619
- Total Carbohydrate: 20.1

147. Mom's Candied Yams With Caramel

Serving: 6 | Prep: 15mins | Ready in:

Ingredients

- 1 (15 ounce) can sweet potatoes, drained and mashed
- 1 (8 ounce) can crushed pineapple, drained
- 3 tablespoons butter
- 2 tablespoons brown sugar
- 1/4 teaspoon salt
- 1 egg, beaten
- 1/2 teaspoon ground cinnamon
- 4 ounces caramel topping
- 2 cups marshmallows, divided

Direction

- Set the oven to 175°C or 350°F to preheat.
- In a bowl, combine together cinnamon, egg, salt, brown sugar, butter, pineapple and sweet potatoes, then pour into a 9-inch x9-inch casserole dish with half of the sweet potato mixture. Drizzle sweet potatoes with caramel sauce, then put 1 cup of marshmallow on top. Spread over marshmallow layer with leftover sweet potato mixture.
- In the preheated oven, bake for half an hour. Put in leftover 1 cup of marshmallows and

bake for 10 minutes longer, until marshmallows turn golden brown.

Nutrition Information

- Calories: 273 calories;
- Protein: 2.7
- Total Fat: 6.8
- Sodium: 274
- Total Carbohydrate: 51.3
- Cholesterol: 46

148. Mom's Green Bean Vegetable Casserole

Serving: 8 | Prep: 5mins | Ready in:

Ingredients

- 1 (10.75 ounce) can condensed cream of celery soup
- 1/2 cup sour cream
- 3/4 cup shredded Cheddar cheese
- 1/2 cup chopped onion
- 1 pinch salt
- 1 (14.5 ounce) can French cut green beans, drained
- 1 (15.25 ounce) can whole kernel corn, drained
- 2 sleeves buttery round crackers, crushed
- 1/2 cup melted butter

Direction

- Set oven to 350°F (175°C) to preheat. Lightly oil a casserole dish.
- Whisk salt, onion, Cheddar cheese, sour cream, and cream of celery soup together in a bowl until well mixed. Stir corn and green beans together in the prepared casserole dish, and distribute the soup mixture over the vegetables. Combine crushed crackers and butter in a bowl. Scatter the crumbs over the top of the casserole.

- Bake for about 45 minutes in the preheated oven until casserole bubbly and surface turns golden brown.

Nutrition Information

- Calories: 406 calories;
- Total Fat: 28.1
- Sodium: 993
- Total Carbohydrate: 33.2
- Cholesterol: 52
- Protein: 7.5

149. Mother In Law Eggs

Serving: 12 | Prep: 15mins | Ready in:

Ingredients

- 6 eggs
- 2 tablespoons mayonnaise
- 1 tablespoon spicy brown mustard (such as Gulden's®)
- 1 teaspoon hot mustard (such as Sweet Hot Mister Mustard®)
- 1 teaspoon white sugar
- salt and pepper to taste
- paprika for garnish (optional)
- 6 pimento-stuffed green olives, cut in half

Direction

- In a saucepan, lay eggs in a single layer and add water to cover by 1 inch. Cover the saucepan and bring to a boil over high heat. Remove from the heat and allow the eggs to sit for 15 minutes in the hot water. Strain. Run cold water over eggs to cool. Remove eggshells once cold. Cut the eggs in half lengthways and remove the yolks to a bowl. Use a fork to mash egg yolks.
- Stir into the yolks with pepper, salt, sugar, hot mustard, spicy brown mustard, and mayonnaise till well mixed. In a quart-size

plastic zip bag, add yolk mixture. On one corner of the plastic bag, cut a small hole.
- Pipe into the egg halves with yolk mixture, use paprika to dredge over each stuffed egg, and lay an olive half on top.

Nutrition Information

- Calories: 57 calories;
- Sodium: 158
- Total Carbohydrate: 0.8
- Cholesterol: 93
- Protein: 3.3
- Total Fat: 4.6

150. Muffin Tin Potatoes Gratin

Serving: 12 | Prep: 10mins | Ready in:

Ingredients

- cooking spray
- 2 tablespoons butter
- 3 cloves garlic, minced
- 2 tablespoons all-purpose flour
- 3/4 cup milk
- 1/2 cup freshly grated Parmesan cheese
- salt and ground black pepper to taste
- 2 large potatoes, peeled and thinly sliced

Direction

- To preheat: set oven to 200°C (400°F). Use cooking spray to spray 12 muffin cups or use butter to grease the 12 muffin cups.
- Add butter to a saucepan then heat on medium heat. Cook and stir garlic in the melted butter for about a minute till you can smell the fragrance. Put flour in the garlic mixture; cook and stir for about 2 minutes till the mixture thickens and becomes smooth.
- Add milk slowly to the flour-butter mixture while using a whisk to stir constantly for approximately 5 minutes till the sauce thickens and becomes smooth. Take the saucepan off heat then stir Parmesan cheese into sauce till cheese is melted by the heat of the sauce, use salt and pepper to season.
- Split the same amount of potatoes to the 12 prepared muffin cups then scoop with the cheese sauce on top.
- Put the muffin cups into the preheated oven and bake for about 25 minutes till potatoes become soft.

Nutrition Information

- Calories: 92 calories;
- Cholesterol: 9
- Protein: 3.2
- Total Fat: 3.3
- Sodium: 88
- Total Carbohydrate: 12.8

151. Mushroom Cream Gravy Sauce

Serving: 6 | Prep: 15mins | Ready in:

Ingredients

- 3 tablespoons butter
- 2 shallots, minced
- 2 cloves garlic, minced
- 1 (4 ounce) package sliced button mushrooms
- 1 tablespoon minced fresh rosemary
- 6 tablespoons white wine, divided
- 1 cup heavy cream
- sea salt to taste
- ground black pepper to taste
- 1 teaspoon grated Parmesan cheese, or to taste (optional)

Direction

- In a heavy-bottomed pan, warm butter over medium heat until foamy; stir and cook garlic

and shallots in the melted butter for about three minutes. Add in rosemary and mushrooms and stir for about 1 minute to coat.
- Mix in 1/4 cup of white wine into the previously prepared mushroom mixture, stir and cook for about 3-5 minutes, or until the mushrooms have become golden brown. Turn up heat to medium high and add 2 tablespoons of white wine and cream. Stir and cook mixture for about five minutes or until the gravy has become thick and creamy. Season gravy with salt and pepper, then drizzle with Parmesan cheese.

Nutrition Information

- Calories: 220 calories;
- Protein: 2.1
- Total Fat: 20.6
- Sodium: 119
- Total Carbohydrate: 5.4
- Cholesterol: 70

152. Nanny's Grape Salad

Serving: 8 | Prep: 15mins | Ready in:

Ingredients

- 1 cup chopped pecans
- 1/3 cup white sugar
- 1 (8 ounce) package cream cheese, softened
- 1 teaspoon vanilla extract
- 2 pounds red seedless grapes

Direction

- In a skillet, cook and stir pecans over medium-low heat for 3-5 minutes till pecans are fragrant and toasted. Take away from the heat and transfer into a heatproof bowl. Stir to avoid overcooking the nuts.
- Use an electric mixer to beat vanilla extract, cream cheese and sugar together in a bowl till

smooth. Fold in grapes and pecans. Gently stir to coat the grapes.

Nutrition Information

- Calories: 306 calories;
- Total Fat: 20.2
- Sodium: 85
- Total Carbohydrate: 31.2
- Cholesterol: 31
- Protein: 4.1

153. No Cook Cranberry Salad

Serving: 8 | Prep: 10mins | Ready in:

Ingredients

- 1 (14.5 ounce) can whole cranberry sauce (such as Ocean Spray®)
- 6 seedless green grapes, halved
- 1/4 (11 ounce) can mandarin oranges, drained and quartered
- 2 tablespoons sweetened flaked coconut
- 1/2 teaspoon vanilla extract
- 1/2 cup chopped walnuts
- 1 red apple, diced

Direction

- In a bowl, blend apple, walnuts, vanilla, coconut, mandarin oranges, grapes and cranberry sauce together. Let the mixture set for half an hour before serving.

Nutrition Information

- Calories: 142 calories;
- Protein: 1.3
- Total Fat: 5.3
- Sodium: 15
- Total Carbohydrate: 24.2
- Cholesterol: 0

154. Nutmeg Mashed Potatoes

Serving: 6 | Prep: 10mins | Ready in:

Ingredients

- 4 large potatoes
- 1/4 cup butter
- 2 teaspoons ground nutmeg, or to taste
- 2 teaspoons salt, or to taste
- 1/2 cup sour cream

Direction

- In a big pot, add potatoes and salted water to cover, then bring water to a boil. Lower heat to moderately low and simmer for 20 minutes, until potatoes are soft and split open. Drain potatoes and turn them back to pot.
- Use a fork or potato masher to mash together salt, nutmeg, butter and potatoes until well-blended, and then stir in sour cream until you get creamy mashed potatoes.

Nutrition Information

- Calories: 304 calories;
- Sodium: 801
- Total Carbohydrate: 44.3
- Cholesterol: 29
- Protein: 5.7
- Total Fat: 12.3

155. Outrageously Good Holiday Salad

Serving: 8 | Prep: 30mins | Ready in:

Ingredients

- 4 red grapefruit, peeled and sectioned
- 1 (8 ounce) package baby salad greens
- 2 bunches green onions, thinly sliced
- 3 avocados - peeled, pitted and sliced
- 8 ounces shredded Swiss cheese
- 1 cup poppy seed salad dressing (such as Marie's®)

Direction

- Drain the grapefruit sections and remove excess juice. Gently mix Swiss cheese, avocados, green onions and salad greens with grapefruit sections. Just before serving, toss dressing with salad.

Nutrition Information

- Calories: 470 calories;
- Sodium: 288
- Total Carbohydrate: 36.4
- Cholesterol: 37
- Protein: 11.6
- Total Fat: 31.9

156. Oven Roasted Turkey Breast

Serving: 6 | Prep: 15mins | Ready in:

Ingredients

- 1/4 cup butter, softened
- 1 clove garlic, minced
- 1 teaspoon paprika
- 1 teaspoon Italian seasoning
- 1/2 teaspoon salt-free garlic and herb seasoning blend (such as Mrs. Dash®)
- salt and ground black pepper to taste
- 1 (3 pound) turkey breast with skin
- 1 teaspoon minced shallot
- 1 tablespoon butter
- 1 splash dry white wine
- 1 cup chicken stock
- 3 tablespoons all-purpose flour
- 2 tablespoons half-and-half (optional)

Direction

- Preheat the oven to 175°C or 350°F.
- In a bowl, combine black pepper, salt, garlic and herb seasoning, Italian seasoning, paprika, garlic and 1/4 cup butter. Into a roasting pan, put the turkey breast, skin side facing up. Using your fingers, loosen the skin; brush on turkey breast and beneath skin with half of butter mixture. Set the rest of butter mixture aside. Loosely tent breast of turkey using aluminum foil.
- In the prepped oven, roast for an hour; with the rest of butter mixture, baste the breast. Put back to oven and roast for an additional of 30 minutes till juices run clear and an inserted instant-read meat thermometer into the chunkiest breast part without touching the bone registers 65°C or 165°F. Allow the turkey breast to sit for 10 to 15 minutes prior to serving.
- Meanwhile, pour pan drippings into a skillet. Remove extra oil, retaining approximately a tablespoon in the skillet. Over low heat, set the skillet; in turkey grease, cook and mix shallot for 5 minutes till opaque. In skillet with shallot, liquify a tablespoon butter and mix in white wine, scratching any food browned bits from skillet. Mix in flour and chicken stock till smooth. Simmer, mixing continuously, till thickened. Mix in half-and-half to have a lighter, creamier gravy.

Nutrition Information

- Calories: 385 calories;
- Sodium: 314
- Total Carbohydrate: 4.3
- Cholesterol: 191
- Protein: 60.3
- Total Fat: 11.8

157. Parmesan Baskets

Serving: 24 | Prep: 10mins | Ready in:

Ingredients

- 8 ounces freshly grated Parmesan cheese, divided

Direction

- Preheat the oven to 175°C or 350°Fahrenheit.
- In a silicone sheet or parchment paper-lined baking sheet, put 2 tsp. of Parmesan cheese then spread gently into a 2-in diameter circle. Make more cheese circles on the sheet at least an inch apart from each other.
- Bake for 4-5 minutes in the preheated oven until golden brown, keep an eye on them to prevent burning. Take it out of the oven; cool on the sheets just until warm. Set the wafers on top of a small bowl or another container while still warm; cool. Store in an airtight container at room temperature.

Nutrition Information

- Calories: 39 calories;
- Sodium: 161
- Total Carbohydrate: 0.3
- Cholesterol: 7
- Total Fat: 2.6
- Protein: 3.6

158. Parmesan Pull Aparts

Serving: 8 | Prep: 10mins | Ready in:

Ingredients

- 3 tablespoons melted butter
- 1/4 teaspoon dill weed
- 1/4 teaspoon celery seed
- 1/4 teaspoon minced onion
- 1 tablespoon grated Parmesan cheese

- 1 (10 ounce) can refrigerated biscuit dough, separated and cut into half circles
- 1 tablespoon grated Parmesan cheese

Direction

- Preheat an oven to 220°C or 425°F.
- Into the base of one 9-inch pie dish, put the melted butter; tilt dish to evenly coat.
- In small bowl, stir 1 tablespoon of the Parmesan cheese, onion, celery seed and dill; pour into pie dish.
- In the pie dish middle, put one biscuit half; put the rest of the biscuit halves around the middle biscuit in clockwise setting. Scatter a tablespoon of Parmesan cheese over biscuits.
- In the prepped oven, bake for 15 to 18 minutes till biscuits turn golden brown. Invert the dish to plate and separate to serve.

Nutrition Information

- Calories: 157 calories;
- Total Carbohydrate: 15.3
- Cholesterol: 13
- Protein: 2.9
- Total Fat: 9.5
- Sodium: 400

159. Pear Honey Cranberry Sauce

Serving: 10 | Prep: 15mins | Ready in:

Ingredients

- 1/2 cup water
- 1/2 cup white sugar
- 2 pears - peeled, cored and diced
- 1 (12 ounce) package fresh or frozen cranberries
- 1 cup honey
- 1 tablespoon fresh lemon juice
- 1 teaspoon grated lemon zest

Direction

- Set a medium pot on medium-high heat, stir in sugar and water then boil; stir in pears then turn the heat down medium heat. Cook for 3mins while frequently stirring; then mix in honey and cranberries. Cook for 5mins until the mixture is slightly thick and the cranberries pop.
- Take off heat then stir the zest and juice of lemon in; cool the mixture to room temperature. Refrigerate, covered, for up to a week.

Nutrition Information

- Calories: 177 calories;
- Cholesterol: 0
- Protein: 0.4
- Total Fat: 0.1
- Sodium: 2
- Total Carbohydrate: 47.3

160. Pecan Cranberry Butter Tarts

Serving: 15 | Prep: 20mins | Ready in:

Ingredients

- 1 cup brown sugar
- 1/2 cup chopped pecans
- 1/2 cup chopped dried cranberries
- 1/3 cup butter, melted
- 1/2 orange, zested and juiced
- 1 egg, beaten
- 1 teaspoon brandy, or to taste
- 15 (2 inch) sweetened pastry tart shells
- 15 pecan halves
- 15 fresh cranberries

Direction

- Set oven to preheat at 350°F (175°C).

- Mix together the brandy, egg, dried cranberries, butter, orange zest, orange juice, chopped pecans, and brown sugar in a bowl.
- Place the tart shells onto a baking sheet and scoop pecan-cranberry filling into each shell filling about 2/3 full. Into each tart, add 1 pecan half and 1 fresh cranberry.
- In the preheated oven, bake till filling bubbly and tart shells turn light brown, for about 18 to 20 minutes.

Nutrition Information

- Calories: 273 calories;
- Total Carbohydrate: 33.9
- Cholesterol: 23
- Protein: 2.8
- Total Fat: 14.6
- Sodium: 109

161. Pecan Pie Cookies

Serving: 24 | Prep: 20mins | Ready in:

Ingredients

- 1/4 cup butter
- 1/2 cup confectioners' sugar
- 3 tablespoons light corn syrup
- 3/4 cup finely chopped pecans
- 2 cups all-purpose flour
- 1 teaspoon baking powder
- 1 cup brown sugar, packed
- 3/4 cup butter, softened
- 1 egg
- 1 teaspoon vanilla extract

Direction

- In a pot, melt a quarter cup of butter; mix in corn syrup and confectioners' sugar until the sugar dissolves. On medium heat, boil the mixture while mixing often; mix in pecans until well blended. Chill the mixture for half an hour.
- Preheat the oven to 175°C or 350°Fahrenheit. In a bowl, sift baking powder and flour together; set aside.
- Using an electric mixer on medium speed, beat vanilla extract, egg, 3/4 cup butter and brown sugar for 2 minutes in a big bowl until the mixture is creamy. Mix in the flour mixture gradually until well combined. Pinch and roll a tbsp. of dough into a ball.
- Press the dough into the bottom of an ungreased cupcake pan cup. With your thumb, push the dough to make a small piecrust shape with 1/4 inch walls up the sides of the cupcake cup. Repeat with the remaining dough. Place a teaspoon of the prepared pecan to fill each little crust.
- Bake for 10-13 minutes in the preheated oven until the cookie shells are pale brown. Watch carefully after 10 minutes. Cool the cookies for 5 minutes in the cupcake pans; completely cool on a wire rack.

Nutrition Information

- Calories: 185 calories;
- Total Fat: 10.4
- Sodium: 82
- Total Carbohydrate: 22.1
- Cholesterol: 28
- Protein: 1.7

162. Perfect Turkey Gravy

Serving: 15 | Prep: 5mins | Ready in:

Ingredients

- 2 (.87 ounce) packages McCormick® Turkey Gravy Mix
- 1/4 cup flour
- 3 cups water
- 1 cup turkey pan drippings or turkey broth

- 1 cup cooked, chopped turkey giblets (optional)

Direction

- In a big saucepan, combine flour and Gravy Mix. Using a wire whisk, slowly mix in turkey drippings and water until smooth. Mix in chopped turkey giblets if you want.
- Whisking often, cook on medium-high heat until the gravy boils. Lower the heat to low, simmer until thickened, or about 5 minutes, whisking sometimes. (The gravy will keep thickening when standing).

Nutrition Information

- Calories: 39 calories;
- Total Carbohydrate: 3.4
- Cholesterol: 28
- Protein: 2.3
- Total Fat: 1.2
- Sodium: 276

163. Pineapple Cranberry Relish

Serving: 10 | Prep: 15mins | Ready in:

Ingredients

- 1 (20 ounce) can crushed pineapple, drained
- 2 (16 ounce) cans whole cranberry sauce
- 1/2 cup chopped walnuts
- 1 (16 ounce) package frozen strawberries, thawed and drained

Direction

- Mix strawberries, pineapple, walnuts, and cranberry sauce in a large bowl. Cover the bowl and let it chill overnight. Serve.

Nutrition Information

- Calories: 216 calories;
- Sodium: 21
- Total Carbohydrate: 47
- Cholesterol: 0
- Protein: 1.3
- Total Fat: 3.9

164. Pomegranate Cranberry Sauce/Relish

Serving: 8 | Prep: 10mins | Ready in:

Ingredients

- 1 pound cranberries
- 1 (16 fl oz) bottle pomegranate juice (such as POM® Wonderful)
- 1 1/2 cups white sugar
- 1/2 cup chopped walnuts (optional)

Direction

- In a saucepan, place the cranberries and pour in pomegranate juice. Cover the pan and bring to a boil until the cranberries start to pop. Adjust the heat to medium. Stir in sugar into cranberry mixture and cook for about 5 minutes, mashing the cranberries constantly with a potato masher or spoon until they have broken. Cover the pan again and adjust the heat to low. Simmer for 2-3 minutes until the sugar is dissolved completely. Mix in walnuts. Before serving, transfer the mixture into a serving dish and let it chill first.

Nutrition Information

- Calories: 259 calories;
- Cholesterol: 0
- Protein: 1.3
- Total Fat: 4.8
- Sodium: 4
- Total Carbohydrate: 55.3

165. Potato Pancakes II

Serving: 3 | Prep: 5mins | Ready in:

Ingredients

- 2 cups mashed potatoes
- 1 egg, beaten
- 1 teaspoon salt
- 1/4 cup shredded Cheddar cheese
- 1 tablespoon butter

Direction

- Combine cheese, salt, beaten egg, and potatoes in a medium mixing bowl. Heat butter on a large griddle at medium heat until melted. Drop 1/4 cup of potato mixture at a time onto the griddle. Use a spatula to flatten to 1/2-inch thick. Fry both sides until golden brown, about 5 minutes per side. Serve right away

Nutrition Information

- Calories: 254 calories;
- Cholesterol: 83
- Protein: 7.2
- Total Fat: 14.5
- Sodium: 1350
- Total Carbohydrate: 23.9

166. Potato Waffles

Serving: 4 | Prep: 10mins | Ready in:

Ingredients

- 2 tablespoons butter
- 1 onion, chopped
- 1 tablespoon minced garlic
- 2 cups mashed potatoes
- 1/4 cup all-purpose flour
- 2 eggs
- 1/4 teaspoon salt
- 1/4 teaspoon ground black pepper

Direction

- In a skillet, melt butter over medium heat.
- Add garlic and onion, stir-fry in melted butter for 5-7 minutes until onion is tender.
- Follow manufacturer's instruction to preheat a waffle iron.
- In a large mixing bowl, mix black pepper, salt, eggs, flour, mashed potatoes, and onion mixture together until well combined.
- Spoon 1/4 - 1/2 cup batter (depending on the waffle iron's size) into the center of the waffle iron and put the lid on. Cook for 3-5 minutes until golden brown.

Nutrition Information

- Calories: 217 calories;
- Total Fat: 9
- Sodium: 540
- Total Carbohydrate: 27.9
- Cholesterol: 110
- Protein: 6.5

167. Potato And Parsnip Gratin

Serving: 6 | Prep: 15mins | Ready in:

Ingredients

- 3 Yukon Gold potatoes, peeled
- 2 parsnips, peeled
- 2 cloves garlic, minced
- 1 tablespoon butter, melted
- salt and ground black pepper to taste
- 1 teaspoon fresh thyme leaves, divided
- 2 ounces finely grated Parmigiano-Reggiano cheese, divided
- 3/4 cup creme fraiche, divided
- 1 cup chicken broth

- 1 pinch cayenne pepper, or to taste

Direction

- In a bowl with cold water, put the parsnips and potatoes.
- Preheat an oven to 190 °C or 375 °F. Into a 2-quart baking dish, put the melted butter and garlic; brush the entire inside of the dish with butter and garlic.
- With a mandoline slicer, cut potatoes very thin.
- Into the bottom of prepped baking dish, arrange 1/3 of slices of potato. Add black pepper and salt to season. Onto slices of potato, scatter several thyme leaves and dust lightly with Parmigiano-Reggiano cheese. Scoop approximately 3 tablespoons of crème fraiche on top of cheese.
- With a vegetable peeler, slice the parsnips thinly; set half the slices of parsnip in an evenly layer on top of crème fraiche and add black pepper and salt to season. Repeat parsnip and potato layering procedure: one third slices of potato, black pepper and salt, the thyme, the Parmigiano-Reggiano cheese, the crème fraiche, and the leftover half slices of parsnip. Sprinkle with salt. Set final 1/3 slices of potato over and put salt to season.
- Top potato-parsnip layers with chicken broth approximately 3 tablespoons at a time. Shake dish gently to get rid of air bubbles. Spread gently the leftover 2 tablespoons crème fraiche on top of potatoes. Over the top, scatter the rest of the Parmigiano-Reggiano cheese and cayenne.
- In the middle of prepped oven, let it bake for 45 minutes up to an hour till gratin turns brown and a knife inserts layers effortlessly.

Nutrition Information

- Calories: 212 calories;
- Protein: 6.2
- Total Fat: 16
- Sodium: 358
- Total Carbohydrate: 12.9

- Cholesterol: 55

168. Pretzel Topped Sweet Potatoes

Serving: 12 | Prep: 20mins | Ready in:

Ingredients

- 13 pretzel rods, crushed
- 1 cup chopped pecans
- 1 cup fresh cranberries
- 1 cup packed light brown sugar
- 1 cup melted butter, divided
- 1 (32 ounce) can sweet potatoes, drained
- 1 (5 ounce) can evaporated milk
- 1/2 cup white sugar
- 1 teaspoon vanilla extract

Direction

- Start preheating the oven to 350°F (175°C). Oil a 9x13-in. baking dish.
- In a bowl, mix together 1/2 cup melted butter, brown sugar, cranberries, pecans, and pretzels.
- In a bowl, whisk sweet potatoes together until smooth; add the leftover 1/2 cup melted butter, vanilla extract, sugar, and evaporated milk and stir until smooth. Ladle the mixture into the prepared baking dish, sprinkle over the top with the pretzel mixture.
- Put in the preheated oven and bake for 25-30 minutes until the edges are bubbly.

Nutrition Information

- Calories: 428 calories;
- Sodium: 387
- Total Carbohydrate: 53.5
- Cholesterol: 44
- Protein: 4.2
- Total Fat: 23.3

169. Pumpkin Bisque (Dairy Free)

Serving: 6 | Prep: 10mins | Ready in:

Ingredients

- 2 tablespoons olive oil
- 1/2 large white onion, chopped
- 2 (15 ounce) cans pumpkin puree
- 1 (13 ounce) can coconut milk
- 2 cups low-sodium chicken broth, or to taste
- 2 tablespoons chopped fresh thyme
- 1 tablespoon sea salt
- 1 teaspoon paprika
- 1 teaspoon garlic powder
- 1 teaspoon herbes de Provence

Direction

- In big pot, heat olive oil on medium heat. Mix and cook onion in hot oil for 5-10 minutes till translucent and soft. Mix coconut milk and pumpkin puree; put broth in till you get desired consistency.
- Mix herbes de Provence, garlic powder, paprika, salt and thyme into pumpkin mixture; boil. Lower heat to low. Simmer for 45 minutes – 1 hour till flavors merge.

Nutrition Information

- Calories: 225 calories;
- Total Fat: 18.2
- Sodium: 1269
- Total Carbohydrate: 15.4
- Cholesterol: 1
- Protein: 4.2

170. Pumpkin Chipotle Pasta Sauce

Serving: 4 | Prep: 10mins | Ready in:

Ingredients

- 1 tablespoon unsalted butter
- 3 tablespoons minced sweet onion
- 1 clove garlic, minced
- 1 cup chicken broth
- 1 cup pumpkin puree
- 2 chipotle peppers in adobo sauce, chopped
- 1/3 cup low-fat milk
- 1 teaspoon ground sage
- 3/4 teaspoon salt
- 1/4 teaspoon ground coriander
- 1 pinch ground cinnamon
- 1 pinch ground nutmeg

Direction

- In a saucepan, melt butter over medium heat, and cook and mix garlic and onion for 3 minutes till onion is translucent. Mix in chicken broth, and boil; mix in chipotle peppers, pumpkin puree and sauce, nutmeg, cinnamon, coriander, salt, sage and milk. Let the sauce come to a simmer, then reduce heat to keep at a simmer till serving.

Nutrition Information

- Calories: 69 calories;
- Sodium: 867
- Total Carbohydrate: 8.1
- Cholesterol: 10
- Protein: 1.9
- Total Fat: 3.6

171. Pumpkin Dump Cake

Serving: 12 | Prep: 10mins | Ready in:

Ingredients

- 1 (29 ounce) can pumpkin puree
- 3 eggs
- 1/2 cup packed brown sugar
- 1/2 cup white sugar
- 1 (12 fluid ounce) can evaporated milk
- 1 teaspoon ground cinnamon
- 1/2 teaspoon ground ginger
- 1/4 teaspoon ground cloves
- 1/2 teaspoon salt
- 1 (18.25 ounce) package spice cake mix
- 1/2 cup coarsely chopped pecans
- 1/2 cup melted butter

Direction

- Start preheating the oven at 350°F (175°C). Grease a 9x13-inch pan.
- In a large bowl, mix milk, white sugar, brown sugar, eggs, and pumpkin purée. Blend in salt, cloves, ginger, and cinnamon. Transfer into the pan. Scatter dry cake mix evenly over the pumpkin filling. Scatter over the cake mix with pecans. Sprinkle melted butter over all.
- Bake in the preheated oven about 50 to 60 minutes, until the edges turn to lightly browned. Let chill.

Nutrition Information

- Calories: 434 calories;
- Total Carbohydrate: 58.4
- Cholesterol: 76
- Protein: 7.6
- Total Fat: 20.1
- Sodium: 658

172. Pumpkin Pie Cake II

Serving: 18 | Prep: 20mins | Ready in:

Ingredients

- 1 (29 ounce) can pumpkin
- 1 (12 fluid ounce) can evaporated milk
- 1 cup white sugar
- 3 eggs
- 3 teaspoons ground cinnamon
- 1 teaspoon salt
- 1 (18.25 ounce) package yellow cake mix
- 3/4 cup butter, melted
- 1 cup chopped pecans

Direction

- Preheat an oven to 175°C/350°F; grease 9x13-in. baking pan lightly.
- Mix salt, cinnamon, eggs, sugar, evaporated milk and pumpkin in a medium bowl. Put it into baking dish. Sprinkle cake mix on pumpkin mixture. Drizzle butter; put pecans over.
- In preheated oven, bake for 50-60 minutes; before serving, cool.

Nutrition Information

- Calories: 333 calories;
- Total Fat: 18
- Sodium: 408
- Total Carbohydrate: 40.3
- Cholesterol: 58
- Protein: 5.2

173. Pumpkin Pie Cocktail

Serving: 1 | Prep: 5mins | Ready in:

Ingredients

- 2 scoops vanilla ice cream
- 1/2 cup crushed ice
- 1 tablespoon canned pumpkin
- 1 fluid ounce half-and-half
- 1 fluid ounce spiced rum
- 1/4 teaspoon pumpkin pie spice
- 2 tablespoons whipped topping
- 1 pinch pumpkin pie spice

Direction

- In a blender, combine 1/4 tsp of pumpkin pie spice, rum, half-and-half, pumpkin, ice and ice cream together. Blend till smooth. Transfer into a serving glass. Place whipped topping and drizzle a pinch of pumpkin pie spice on top.

Nutrition Information

174. Pumpkin Pie French Toast

Serving: 4 | Prep: 15mins | Ready in:

Ingredients

- 3 large eggs
- 1/2 cup half-and-half cream
- 1/4 cup canned pumpkin puree
- 1 teaspoon ground cinnamon
- 1 teaspoon vanilla extract
- 1/4 teaspoon pumpkin pie spice
- 1/4 cup finely chopped walnuts
- 8 slices day-old bread

Direction

- Heat on medium heat with a lightly oiled skillet.
- In a bowl, whisk together walnuts, pumpkin pie spice, vanilla extract, cinnamon, pumpkin, half-and-half and eggs. Steep in the pumpkin mixture with a bread slice at a time, then arrange in the prepared skillet. Repeat process with the leftover bread slices. Stir the pumpkin mixture between dips to prevent walnuts from settling. Cook the slices of bread for 3 minutes per side, until turning golden brown.

Nutrition Information

- Calories: 284 calories;
- Sodium: 443
- Total Carbohydrate: 29.8
- Cholesterol: 151
- Protein: 10.7
- Total Fat: 13.7

175. Pumpkin Pie Soup

Serving: 6 | Prep: 25mins | Ready in:

Ingredients

- 4 pounds pumpkin, peeled and cut into cubes
- 2 cups vanilla-flavored coconut beverage
- 1 (14.5 ounce) can chicken broth
- 4 teaspoons ground cinnamon
- 2 teaspoons ground ginger
- 1 teaspoon ground cloves
- 1/2 teaspoon dried sage
- 1/2 teaspoon salt
- 1/2 cup vanilla yogurt (optional)
- chopped toasted walnuts (optional)

Direction

- Preheat an oven to 200°C/400°F. Line foil on a baking sheet; roast pumpkin for 45 minutes till tender.
- Boil salt, sage, cloves, ginger, cinnamon, chicken broth, coconut beverage and pumpkin in a stockpot. Lower the heat; simmer for 5 minutes. Use an immersion blender/hand mixer to blend the soup till smooth; serve with a dollop of yogurt and sprinkling of nuts (optional).

Nutrition Information

- Calories: 195 calories;
- Total Fat: 9.2
- Sodium: 503
- Total Carbohydrate: 28
- Cholesterol: 3

- Protein: 6.3

176. Pumpkin Popovers

Serving: 6 | Prep: 15mins | Ready in:

Ingredients

- 1 cup milk
- 2 eggs
- 1/4 cup pumpkin puree
- 1 tablespoon vegetable oil
- 1 cup all-purpose flour
- 1 tablespoon brown sugar
- 1/2 teaspoon pumpkin pie spice
- 1/2 teaspoon salt

Direction

- Preheat the oven to 175°C or 350°Fahrenheit. Slather butter in four muffin cups or custard dishes.
- With an electric mixer, whisk eggs and milk together in a bowl until smooth; stir in oil and pumpkin. Whisk in salt, flour, pumpkin pie spice, and brown sugar until it turns into a smooth batter. Scoop batter in buttered cups until half full.
- Bake popovers for 20-25mins in a 350°Fahrenheit oven until the surface is pale brown.

Nutrition Information

- Calories: 153 calories;
- Total Fat: 5
- Sodium: 260
- Total Carbohydrate: 21.1
- Cholesterol: 65
- Protein: 5.7

177. Pumpkin Smoothie

Serving: 4 | Prep: 5mins | Ready in:

Ingredients

- 1 (16 ounce) can pumpkin puree
- 2 cups milk
- 1/4 cup brown sugar
- 2 teaspoons ground cinnamon

Direction

- In a freezer bag, add pumpkin puree and keep in the freezer for a minimum of 1 day.
- Microwave the bag of pumpkin puree on high setting for 1-2 minutes, until softened.
- Add in the blender with milk, then put in pumpkin, cinnamon and brown sugar then blend until smooth.

Nutrition Information

- Calories: 155 calories;
- Total Fat: 2.7
- Sodium: 328
- Total Carbohydrate: 29.3
- Cholesterol: 10
- Protein: 5.3

178. Pumpkin Soup The Easy Way

Serving: 16 | Prep: 20mins | Ready in:

Ingredients

- 1 tablespoon butter
- 1 cup chopped onion
- 2 teaspoons minced garlic
- 2 pounds cubed fully cooked ham
- 3 (29 ounce) cans pumpkin puree
- 1 (32 ounce) carton chicken broth
- 2/3 cup cream

- 1 teaspoon fresh thyme
- 1 teaspoon ground black pepper
- 1/2 teaspoon fresh rosemary

Direction

- In a skillet, melt butter on medium heat. Cook the garlic and onion in butter till tender.
- In the slow cook that's set to Low, mix rosemary, pepper, thyme, cream, chicken broth, pumpkin puree, ham, garlic and onion; cook for 8 - 10 hours.

Nutrition Information

- Calories: 241 calories;
- Sodium: 1373
- Total Carbohydrate: 14.1
- Cholesterol: 49
- Protein: 12.8
- Total Fat: 15.5

179. Pumpkin Spice Russian

Serving: 1 | Prep: 5mins | Ready in:

Ingredients

- 1/2 cup ice, or as desired
- 1 fluid ounce pumpkin spice-flavored liqueur
- 1 fluid ounce vanilla-flavored vodka
- 1/4 cup half-and-half
- 1 cinnamon stick
- 1 tablespoon whipped cream, or to taste
- 1 pinch pumpkin pie spice

Direction

- Add ice to fill 1/2 of the glass. Pour vanilla-flavored vodka and pumpkin spice-flavored liqueur over ice; add half-and-half on top. Use a cinnamon stick to stir; add pumpkin pie spice and whipped cream for garnish.

Nutrition Information

- Calories: 263 calories;
- Sodium: 35
- Total Carbohydrate: 17.7
- Cholesterol: 25
- Protein: 2
- Total Fat: 7.9

180. Quick Brown Rice And Mushroom Pilaf

Serving: 8 | Prep: | Ready in:

Ingredients

- 2 tablespoons olive oil
- 1 small onion, chopped
- 1/4 cup celery, chopped
- 1 1/2 cups sliced mushrooms
- 1 (14.5 ounce) can chicken broth
- 2 cups Minute® Brown Rice, uncooked
- 1/2 cup chopped walnuts, toasted
- 2 tablespoons fresh parsley, chopped

Direction

- In a medium saucepan, heat oil over medium heat and add the celery and onions, then cook for 3 minutes, stirring sometimes, until tender-crisp.
- Add the mushrooms and cook, occasionally stirring, for 3 minutes until mushrooms become tender. Add the broth, stir, and set to boil.
- Stir in the rice and cover, then bring heat down to medium-low and simmer for 5 minutes. Take off the heat and let sit for 5 minutes. Add parsley and walnuts, lightly mixing.

Nutrition Information

- Calories: 163 calories;

- Cholesterol: 1
- Protein: 3.4
- Total Fat: 9.1
- Sodium: 227
- Total Carbohydrate: 19.7

181. Quick Brussels And Bacon

Serving: 6 | Prep: 15mins | Ready in:

Ingredients

- 6 slices bacon
- 1/2 tablespoon olive oil
- 3 shallots, chopped
- 1 (16 ounce) package frozen Brussels sprouts, thawed and halved

Direction

- On medium-high heat, cook bacon in a big pan until crisp; place on paper towels to drain. Break the bacon into small pieces.
- On medium-high heat, heat olive oil in a big pan; add onion. Cook and stir in the oil until soft; add bacon. Keep on cooking until the bacon is warmed through; add in Brussels sprouts. Cook and stir for 7-10mins until brown.

Nutrition Information

- Calories: 189 calories;
- Total Fat: 14
- Sodium: 255
- Total Carbohydrate: 11.2
- Cholesterol: 19
- Protein: 6.4

182. Quick Caramel Apple Pie

Serving: 8 | Prep: | Ready in:

Ingredients

- 2 (9 inch) unbaked pie shells
- 5 large tart apples, cored and sliced
- 4 tablespoons all-purpose flour
- 1/3 cup packed brown sugar
- 1 cup fat free caramel dip

Direction

- To preheat: Set oven to 190°C (375°F).
- Mix brown sugar and 2 tablespoons flour together. Toss the mixture with apples.
- Use a tablespoon flour to sprinkle on bottom crust, roll lightly to fit a 10 or 9 inch pie pan. Assemble apples in the bottom crust, and pour caramel sauce over apples. Use the remaining flour to roll out the second crust. Lay the crust over apples. Tuck the second crust over the bottom crust and pinch edges together. Make a few holes on top of pie to let steam escape.
- Put pie into the oven and bake for 40 – 45 minutes till pie turns golden brown. Allow pie to cool before serving.

Nutrition Information

- Calories: 450 calories;
- Cholesterol: 0
- Protein: 3.7
- Total Fat: 14.4
- Sodium: 403
- Total Carbohydrate: 78.7

183. Quick Cranberry Butter

Serving: 8 | Prep: 10mins | Ready in:

Ingredients

- 2 tablespoons dried cranberries

- 1/2 cup boiling water
- 1/2 cup butter, softened
- 3 tablespoons confectioners' sugar

Direction

- In a bowl, combine cranberries with boiling water, let soak for 5 minutes. Drain and chop the soaked cranberries.
- Use an electric mixer to cream butter in a bowl until it gets fluffy and light. Mix in cranberries and confectioners' sugar.

Nutrition Information

- Calories: 119 calories;
- Total Fat: 11.5
- Sodium: 82
- Total Carbohydrate: 4.5
- Cholesterol: 31
- Protein: 0.1

184. Quick Cranberry Relish

Serving: 8 | Prep: 15mins | Ready in:

Ingredients

- 1 (12 ounce) package fresh cranberries
- 3/4 cup orange juice
- 1/2 cup raisins
- 1/2 cup white sugar
- 3 cups apples - peeled, cored, and chopped (optional)

Direction

- In a blender or food processor, chop the cranberries.
- In a saucepan, stir together sugar, raisins, orange juice, and cranberries; allow to simmer and cook for 8 - 10 minutes until the cranberries are soft. Let cool. Fold in the apples.

Nutrition Information

- Calories: 133 calories;
- Sodium: 3
- Total Carbohydrate: 34.7
- Cholesterol: 0
- Protein: 0.8
- Total Fat: 0.2

185. Quick Gingerbread Latte

Serving: 1 | Prep: 5mins | Ready in:

Ingredients

- 1/2 cup milk
- 1/2 cup water
- 1 tablespoon white sugar
- 1 tablespoon instant coffee
- 1 pinch ground ginger
- 1 pinch ground cinnamon
- 1 pinch ground cloves
- 1 pinch ground nutmeg
- 1 tablespoon whipped cream, or more to taste

Direction

- In a microwave-safe bowl, put water, milk, coffee, sugar, cinnamon, nutmeg, ginger, and cloves and whisk together. Place bowl inside the microwave and heat for 2 minutes, or until warmed. Transfer latte to a mug; put whipped cream on top.

Nutrition Information

- Calories: 138 calories;
- Total Fat: 3.7
- Sodium: 61
- Total Carbohydrate: 22.2
- Cholesterol: 12
- Protein: 4.7

186. Quick Pumpkin Cake

Serving: 30 | Prep: 10mins | Ready in:

Ingredients

- 1 (18.25 ounce) package yellow cake mix
- 1 (15 ounce) can pumpkin puree
- 1/3 cup vegetable oil
- 2 eggs
- 2 teaspoons pumpkin pie spice
- 3/4 cup cream cheese, softened
- 1/2 cup butter, softened
- 1 tablespoon vanilla extract
- 3 cups confectioners' sugar

Direction

- Preheat an oven to 175°C/350°F; grease 9x13-in. pan.
- Mix pumpkin pie spice, eggs, vegetable oil, pumpkin puree and cake mix in a bowl; put in prepped pan.
- In preheated oven, bake for 20 minutes till inserted toothpick in middle of cake exits clean. Remove from oven; fully cool cake.
- Beat vanilla extract, butter and cream cheese till creamy and light in a bowl; beat confectioners' sugar slowly into mixture till smooth. Spread on cooled cake.

Nutrition Information

- Calories: 201 calories;
- Total Fat: 9.9
- Sodium: 191
- Total Carbohydrate: 26.9
- Cholesterol: 27
- Protein: 1.8

187. Quick Pumpkin Spice Latte

Serving: 1 | Prep: 5mins | Ready in:

Ingredients

- 1 cup milk, divided
- 1 tablespoon white sugar, or more to taste
- 1 tablespoon pumpkin puree
- 1 teaspoon pumpkin pie spice
- 1/2 teaspoon vanilla extract
- 1/4 cup brewed espresso

Direction

- In a small saucepan, whisk vanilla extract, pumpkin pie spice, pumpkin puree, sugar and 1/2 cup of milk over low heat. Simmer for 5 minutes then whisk in the leftover 1/2 cup of milk.
- Discard pulp by pouring milk mixture through a fine-mesh sieve. Bring milk mixture back to the saucepan; simmer and whisk for 2 minutes. Whisk in espresso for 1 minute till foamy.

Nutrition Information

- Calories: 184 calories;
- Total Fat: 5.1
- Sodium: 110
- Total Carbohydrate: 25.4
- Cholesterol: 20
- Protein: 8.2

188. Quick Turkey And Rice

Serving: 6 | Prep: 10mins | Ready in:

Ingredients

- 3 cups water
- 1 1/2 cups uncooked long-grain rice
- 1 tablespoon cooking oil
- 1 cup chopped green bell pepper
- 2 stalks celery, cut into 1 inch pieces
- 1 yellow onion, finely chopped
- 1 pound boneless turkey breast, cut into 1 inch cubes

- 1 (14.5 ounce) can stewed tomatoes, drained

Direction

- Boil water in a saucepan. Put in rice and mix. Lower the heat, place cover on and simmer for 20 minutes.
- In the meantime, in a big skillet, heat the oil over moderately high heat. Sauté the onion, celery and bell pepper for 2 to 3 minutes till soft. Put in the turkey, and keep sautéing till turkey is no longer pink on the outside. Mix in tomatoes, and put cover on. Keep simmering, mixing from time to time, till turkey is cooked completely and not pink anymore on the inside. Serve on top of hot cooked rice.

Nutrition Information

- Calories: 328 calories;
- Total Carbohydrate: 46.8
- Cholesterol: 53
- Protein: 22.8
- Total Fat: 4.9
- Sodium: 198

189. Quick Yeast Rolls

Serving: 8 | Prep: 1hours30mins | Ready in:

Ingredients

- 2 tablespoons shortening
- 3 tablespoons white sugar
- 1 cup hot water
- 1 (.25 ounce) package active dry yeast
- 1 egg, beaten
- 1 teaspoon salt
- 2 1/4 cups all-purpose flour

Direction

- Combine hot water, sugar and shortening in a big bowl. Cool till lukewarm, then stir in yeast till dissolved. Stir in flour, salt and egg. Let dough to rise till doubled in size.
- Oil 8 muffin cups. Split dough among the prepped muffin cups and let rise once more till doubled in size.
- Preheat the oven to 220°C or 425°F.
- In the prepped oven, let bake for 10 minutes, or till a knife pricked in the middle of one muffin comes out clean.

Nutrition Information

- Calories: 186 calories;
- Total Fat: 4.2
- Sodium: 301
- Total Carbohydrate: 31.9
- Cholesterol: 23
- Protein: 4.8

190. Quick And Easy Pumpkin Mousse

Serving: 10 | Prep: 5mins | Ready in:

Ingredients

- 1 tablespoon butter
- 24 marshmallows
- 1/2 cup milk
- 1/2 cup canned pumpkin
- 1 teaspoon vanilla extract
- 1 teaspoon pumpkin pie spice
- 1/3 cup confectioners' sugar
- 1 cup heavy cream

Direction

- In a big fry pan, melt the butter. Stir in the pumpkin, milk and marshmallows. Mix often until it becomes smooth and melted. Take it out of the heat, then mix in pumpkin pie spice and vanilla. Let it fully cool for around half an hour.

- In a big bowl, mix together 1 cup heavy cream and 1/3 cup of confectioner's sugar. Beat it using an electric mixer until it forms stiff peaks. Fold the whipped cream into the cooled pumpkin mixture. Pour the mousse into chocolate shells or ramekins. Put cover and let it chill in the fridge for around 2 hours, until it becomes firm.

Nutrition Information

- Calories: 176 calories;
- Cholesterol: 37
- Protein: 1.4
- Total Fat: 10.3
- Sodium: 37
- Total Carbohydrate: 20.6

191. Quick And Easy Pumpkin Pie Milkshake

Serving: 2 | Prep: 5mins | Ready in:

Ingredients

- 1/4 pumpkin pie
- 6 scoops vanilla ice cream
- 2 tablespoons bourbon (optional)
- 1/2 teaspoon pumpkin pie spice, divided
- 1 cup whole milk
- 2 tablespoons whipped cream, or to taste

Direction

- In a blender, process pumpkin pie with whole milk, ice cream, a quarter tsp pumpkin pie spice, and bourbon until smooth.
- Pour milkshakes into two glasses; add whipped cream and the rest of the pumpkin pie spice on top.

Nutrition Information

- Calories: 284 calories;
- Total Fat: 13.3
- Sodium: 154
- Total Carbohydrate: 25.9
- Cholesterol: 46
- Protein: 6.9

192. Quick And Easy Sausage Stuffing

Serving: 12 | Prep: 10mins | Ready in:

Ingredients

- 1/4 cup butter
- 1 large onion, diced
- 2 apples - peeled, cored, and diced
- 2 (6 ounce) boxes dry stuffing mix
- 2 1/2 cups boiling water, or more if needed
- 1 pound bulk pork sausage

Direction

- Put butter in a skillet and heat it over low heat. Mix in onion and cook for 5 minutes until slightly tender. Add the apples and cook for 5-10 more minutes until they are tender.
- In a bowl with boiling water, whisk in the stuffing mix. Cover the bowl and allow the mixture to sit for 5 minutes until the water is completely absorbed. If the stuffing is too dry, pour in more water.
- Set the large skillet over medium-high heat. Cook and stir the sausage for 5-7 minutes until crumbly and evenly browned. Drain and discard any grease.
- Combine the onion-apple mixture, stuffing, and the sausage.

Nutrition Information

- Calories: 256 calories;
- Total Fat: 13
- Sodium: 817
- Total Carbohydrate: 26.2

- Cholesterol: 32
- Protein: 8.5

193. Quinoa Stuffing

Serving: 8 | Prep: 25mins | Ready in:

Ingredients

- 4 cups vegetable stock
- 2 cups quinoa
- 1/4 cup olive oil
- 1 butternut squash - peeled, seeded, and diced
- 2 small zucchinis, cut into 1-inch cubes
- 1 bunch green onions, chopped
- 1 cup diced dried apricots
- 1 cup dried cranberries
- 1 cup chopped fresh parsley
- 1 lime, juiced, or to taste

Direction

- Allow the vegetable stock to boil in a saucepan, adjusting the heat to low, and add in quinoa; stir. Cover the pan and make it simmer for 10 to 15 minutes until it absorbs the liquid. Take it off from heat.
- Pour the olive oil a big skillet placed over medium heat. Cook zucchinis and butternut squash in the hot oil, giving them a stir until slightly browned, roughly 10 minutes. Mix the quinoa into the vegetables and stir apricots, green onions, parsley and cranberries into the stuffing gently. Sprinkle with lime juice for added savor.

Nutrition Information

- Calories: 387 calories;
- Sodium: 258
- Total Carbohydrate: 70.7
- Cholesterol: 0
- Protein: 9.1
- Total Fat: 9.8

194. Really Easy Bread Stuffing

Serving: 5 | Prep: | Ready in:

Ingredients

- 1 (1 pound) loaf white bread
- 1 small onion, chopped
- 1 teaspoon poultry seasoning
- 1 pinch salt
- 1 pinch ground black pepper
- 1/4 cup water

Direction

- Use as much water as needed to moisten all bread. Add pepper, salt, seasoning and onion. Mix using your hands.
- Put in foil and wrap up or in turkey; cook for at least 1 hour (longer if cooking in the turkey). To make top crusty, open the foil on the final 15 minutes of cooking.

Nutrition Information

- Calories: 248 calories;
- Total Fat: 3
- Sodium: 619
- Total Carbohydrate: 47.6
- Cholesterol: 0
- Protein: 7.1

195. Red Wine Poached Pears With Chocolate Filling

Serving: 6 | Prep: 15mins | Ready in:

Ingredients

- 4 pears, peeled, or more to taste

- 1 1/2 cups red wine
- 1 cup water
- 2/3 cup white sugar
- 2 tablespoons lemon juice
- 2 teaspoons ground cinnamon
- 1 star anise pod (optional)
- 1 (11 ounce) jar chocolate sauce (such as Fran's®)

Direction

- Slice off base of every pear and core from the base, giving every pear a flat base to stand upright.
- In a big saucepan, mix star anise, cinnamon, lemon juice, sugar, water and wine; boil. Lower the heat and place pears in saucepan on their sides. Let pears simmer for 10 minutes to 12 minutes. Flip pears and keep simmering for 8 to 10 minutes, till soft and effortlessly pricked using fork. Do it in batches if necessary.
- Take pears off wine mixture and put, standing upright, in serving dish. Let wine sauce boil for an additional 5 to 10 minutes, till cooked down to roughly 3/4 cup.
- Use chocolate sauce to fill every core cavity of pear. Top each pear with wine sauce.

Nutrition Information

- Calories: 400 calories;
- Sodium: 183
- Total Carbohydrate: 78.7
- Cholesterol: 1
- Protein: 3
- Total Fat: 4.8

196. Renee's Pumpkin Apple Butter

Serving: 40 | Prep: 30mins | Ready in:

Ingredients

- 1 (29 ounce) can pumpkin puree
- 1 cup apple cider
- 1 Granny Smith apple, peeled and chopped
- 1/4 cup unsweetened applesauce
- 1 tablespoon pumpkin pie spice
- 1/4 cup honey
- 2 tablespoons stevia-sugar blend for baking (such as Truvia® Baking Blend)

Direction

- In a skillet, mix the apple, pumpkin pie spice, pumpkin, applesauce, and cider over medium-low heat. Cook and frequently stir the mixture for 10-12 minutes until the pumpkin-apple butter turns thick. Add the stevia-sugar blend and honey.
- Fill the blender with the pumpkin-apple butter halfway. Cover the blender. Use a potholder to hold the lid of the blender down. Pulse the mixture several times before blending it. Place into a container covered with lid. Do the same procedures with the rest of the pumpkin-apple butter.

Nutrition Information

- Calories: 20 calories;
- Total Fat: 0.1
- Sodium: 50
- Total Carbohydrate: 5.4
- Cholesterol: 0
- Protein: 0.2

197. Rich Turkey Gravy

Serving: 6 | Prep: 10mins | Ready in:

Ingredients

- 1/4 cup all-purpose flour, or more if needed
- 1/4 cup turkey drippings
- 2 cups water
- 2 chicken bouillon cubes

Direction

- Mix the flour and turkey drippings together in a skillet over medium heat till smooth, then turn heat down to low and cook for 10 minutes, mixing often, until dark brown. Mix in the bouillon cubes and water, and let simmer for about 10 minutes, till the gravy is thickened and smooth, cubes have dissolved.

Nutrition Information

- Calories: 99 calories;
- Sodium: 386
- Total Carbohydrate: 4.4
- Cholesterol: 9
- Protein: 0.8
- Total Fat: 8.7

198. Roasted Brussels Sprouts With Apples, Golden Raisins, And Walnuts

Serving: 6 | Prep: 15mins | Ready in:

Ingredients

- 1 pound Brussels sprouts, halved
- 1 cup chopped cauliflower
- 2 apples - peeled, cored, and cut into chunks
- 1 sweet onion, sliced
- 1 tablespoon olive oil, or more if needed
- salt and ground black pepper to taste
- 1/2 cup golden raisins
- 1/4 cup chopped walnuts
- 1 tablespoon Chardonnay wine, or more to taste

Direction

- Preheat the oven to 400°F (200 °C). Use an aluminium foil to line baking sheet. On the prepped baking sheet, distribute the onion, apples, cauliflower and Brussels sprouts properly before drizzling olive oil over them. Add black pepper and salt. Coat everything equally by stirring. Put baking sheet into preheated oven. Bake for 20-25 minutes until the cauliflower and sprouts tenderize. Move them in a serving bowl before folding in the walnuts and raisins and drizzling wine over the top. Coat everything by tossing.

Nutrition Information

- Calories: 158 calories;
- Total Fat: 5.8
- Sodium: 27
- Total Carbohydrate: 26.1
- Cholesterol: 0
- Protein: 4.4

199. Roasted Butternut Squash With Onions, Spinach, And Craisins®

Serving: 6 | Prep: 15mins | Ready in:

Ingredients

- 1 butternut squash
- 1 cup chopped red onion
- 2 tablespoons olive oil
- 3 ounces fresh spinach, stems removed and leaves torn in bite-size pieces
- 1/3 cup sweetened dried cranberries (such as Craisins®)
- 1/3 cup chopped pecans (optional)

Direction

- Set the oven to 230°C or 450°F and grease a baking sheet slightly.
- Cut crosswise the butternut squash into slices with 1 inch size. Peel and clean each slice, then get rid of the seeds and stringy pulp from the center. Slice cleaned slices into cubes with 1 inch size.

- In a bowl, toss together olive oil, onion and squash cubes until coated well, then turn out onto the prepared baking sheet.
- In the preheated oven, roast the squash for 25-30 minutes, until softened and beginning to brown.
- In a serving bowl, toss together pecans, dried cranberries, spinach and squash mixture, then serve warm.

Nutrition Information

- Calories: 198 calories;
- Total Fat: 9.5
- Sodium: 19
- Total Carbohydrate: 29.5
- Cholesterol: 0
- Protein: 3

200. Roasted Peppers With Pine Nuts And Parsley

Serving: 10 | Prep: 20mins | Ready in:

Ingredients

- 2 red bell peppers
- 2 yellow bell peppers
- 2 ounces pine nuts
- 1/3 cup golden raisins
- 1 clove garlic, minced
- 1/2 cup chopped fresh parsley
- 1/2 cup olive oil
- salt and ground black pepper to taste

Direction

- Start preheating the oven broiler, put the oven rack at about 6 inches away from the heat source. Use aluminum foil to line a baking sheet. Use a knife to separate peppers in half from top to bottom; remove the ribs, seeds and stem, then on a prepared baking sheets, place the peppers cut sides down. Cook in the oven broiler for about 10 minutes until the peppers skin turn blistered and blackened. In a bowl, place in blackened peppers and cover tightly with plastic wrap. Allow to steam for about 20 minutes while cooling down. When cool, remove and throw away the skin.
- In a small dry skillet, toast pine nuts over medium-low heat, swirl the pine nuts for 1 to 2 minutes until they have nutty scent and turn to light tan color. Remove from the heat, pour into a small bowl in order to avoid overcooking.
- Cut the roasted peppers into strips, and on a serving platter, place peppers strips decoratively by alternating yellow and red ones. Sprinkle peppers with parsley, garlic, raisins and toasted pine nuts. Add in olive oil in a drizzle; put salt and black pepper to season.

Nutrition Information

- Calories: 160 calories;
- Sodium: 4
- Total Carbohydrate: 8.4
- Cholesterol: 0
- Protein: 2.1
- Total Fat: 13.8

201. Roasted Turkey Criolla Marinade

Serving: 20 | Prep: 15mins | Ready in:

Ingredients

- 1/2 cup melted butter
- 1/2 cup olive oil
- 8 cloves garlic
- 1 orange, zested
- 1 tablespoon salt
- 1 teaspoon black peppercorns
- 1 teaspoon chopped fresh oregano
- 1 teaspoon chopped fresh rosemary

- 1 teaspoon chopped fresh thyme
- 1/2 teaspoon ground cumin
- 2 tablespoons balsamic vinegar
- 1/2 cup fresh orange juice
- 2 whole cloves
- 1 small onion
- 1 cinnamon stick
- 1/2 orange
- 1 bay leaf

Direction

- Combine the orange juice, balsamic vinegar, cumin, thyme, rosemary, oregano, peppercorns, salt, orange zest, garlic, olive oil, and butter in a blender. Pulse several times to mix well.
- Insert the cloves into an onion. Place the bay leaf, orange half, cinnamon stick, and clove-spiked onion into the cavity of the turkey. Put turkey in an oven bag. Use fingers to loosen the skin over the breast and legs of the turkey. Pour marinade under the loosened turkey skin. Seal the bag. Roast according to the oven bag instructions based on the weight of the turkey.

Nutrition Information

202. Rosemary Sage Squash Seeds

Serving: 2 | Prep: 10mins | Ready in:

Ingredients

- 1/2 cup squash seeds
- 1 tablespoon olive oil
- 1 teaspoon dried rosemary, or more to taste
- 1/2 teaspoon salt
- 1/4 teaspoon dried sage

Direction

- Set your oven to preheat at 300°F (150°C). Use an aluminum foil to line your baking pan. If you don't have aluminum foil, you can use a parchment paper.
- Clean your squash seeds thoroughly and be sure to separate it from squash flesh. Rinse the seeds by using a fine-mesh strainer and let it dry by spreading it into a paper towel.
- On a clean bowl, mix olive oil, salt, sage, rosemary and the squash seeds and combine well. Transfer the seasoned seeds onto the prepared baking pan and spread in a single layer.
- Let it bake in the preheated oven for about 30-40 minutes or until the seeds are crispy. Be sure to flip the seeds every 10 minutes during baking time.

Nutrition Information

- Calories: 248 calories;
- Sodium: 588
- Total Carbohydrate: 6.5
- Cholesterol: 0
- Protein: 8.5
- Total Fat: 22.7

203. Sally's Spinach Mashed Potatoes

Serving: 8 | Prep: 15mins | Ready in:

Ingredients

- 1 (10 ounce) package frozen chopped spinach
- 6 potatoes, peeled and chopped
- 1/2 cup butter
- 1 cup sour cream
- 1 tablespoon chopped onion
- 1 teaspoon salt
- 1/4 teaspoon dried dill weed
- 1 cup shredded Cheddar cheese

Direction

- Preheat oven to 350° F (175° C). Oil a medium casserole dish lightly.
- Cook spinach as stated by the package directions. In a pot, add potato and cover with enough water, allow to boil. Cook for 15 minutes, up to softened but firm. Let it drain, cool slightly, then mash.
- In a bowl, combine the dill, salt, onion, sour cream, butter, mashed potatoes, and spinach together. Move to the prepped casserole dish. Put Cheddar cheese on top.
- In the preheated oven, bake for 20 minutes until lightly brown and bubbly.

Nutrition Information

- Calories: 354 calories;
- Protein: 9.1
- Total Fat: 22.6
- Sodium: 511
- Total Carbohydrate: 31
- Cholesterol: 58

204. Sarah's Frozen Pumpkin Spice Cocktail

Serving: 2 | Prep: 10mins | Ready in:

Ingredients

- 1/4 cup heavy whipping cream
- 1/4 cup milk
- 1/4 cup pumpkin puree
- 1/4 cup pumpkin spice coffee-flavored liqueur (such as Kahlua®)
- 1/2 teaspoon pumpkin pie spice
- 8 cubes ice cubes

Direction

- In a blender, blend the pumpkin puree, pumpkin pie spice, pumpkin liqueur, cream, milk, and ice for 30-45 seconds until smooth.

Nutrition Information

- Calories: 235 calories;
- Protein: 2
- Total Fat: 11.8
- Sodium: 102
- Total Carbohydrate: 18.2
- Cholesterol: 43

205. Sausage Oyster Dressing

Serving: 12 | Prep: 15mins | Ready in:

Ingredients

- 1 (16 ounce) package bulk mild pork sausage (such as Jimmy Dean®)
- 1 (16 ounce) package bulk hot pork sausage (such as Jimmy Dean®)
- 1 (16 ounce) package plain croutons
- 1 pint shucked oysters, drained with liquid reserved
- 2 cups diced celery
- 2 eggs, beaten
- 1/4 cup chopped onion
- 1 1/2 cups chicken broth, or as needed
- 1/2 cup butter, melted

Direction

- Preheat an oven to 165°C/325°F then grease the 9x13-in. baking dish.
- Put pork sausage in skillet on medium heat; brown sausage, breaking up to crumbles while cooking, for about 10 minutes till sausage isn't pink and is mixed together well. Drain grease. Put sausage into big bowl. Mix onions, eggs, celery, oysters and croutons in till combined well. Mix enough chicken broth and reserved oyster liquid to get 2 cups in bowl. Put into dressing; mix butter in. Put dressing in prepped baking dish.
- In preheated oven, bake for about 30 minutes till oysters are cooked, browned and hot.

Nutrition Information

- Calories: 462 calories;
- Cholesterol: 109
- Protein: 18.8
- Total Fat: 28.1
- Sodium: 1202
- Total Carbohydrate: 32.2

206. Scott's Sweet Potato And Butternut Squash Mashers

Serving: 8 | Prep: 10mins | Ready in:

Ingredients

- 3 sweet potato, peeled and cubed
- 1 butternut squash- peeled, seeded and cubed
- 1/2 teaspoon ground cinnamon
- 1/2 teaspoon nutmeg
- 1/4 cup sugar free maple flavored syrup

Direction

- In a large pot, combine butternut squash and sweet potatoes; pour in enough water to cover. Place over high heat and bring to a boil, then lower the heat to medium low and simmer, covered, for about 20 minutes until softened. Drain off excess water and let steam dry for 1 to 2 minutes.
- Mash the vegetables, then add syrup, nutmeg and cinnamon. Mix until mixture is smooth.

Nutrition Information

- Calories: 145 calories;
- Sodium: 53
- Total Carbohydrate: 35.6
- Cholesterol: 0
- Protein: 2.9
- Total Fat: 0.3

207. Sesame Green Beans

Serving: 4 | Prep: 5mins | Ready in:

Ingredients

- 1 tablespoon olive oil
- 1 tablespoon sesame seeds
- 1 pound fresh green beans, cut into 2 inch pieces
- 1/4 cup chicken broth
- 1/4 teaspoon salt
- freshly ground black pepper to taste

Direction

- In a big skillet or wok, heat oil on medium heat. Put in sesame seeds. Once seeds begin to darken, stir in green beans. Cook and stir until the beans have bright green color.
- Add pepper, salt and chicken broth. Cover and cook for around 10 minutes, until beans are crisp-tender. Uncover and cook until liquid evaporates.

Nutrition Information

- Calories: 78 calories;
- Total Fat: 4.6
- Sodium: 152
- Total Carbohydrate: 8.6
- Cholesterol: 0
- Protein: 2.5

208. Simple Deep Fried Turkey

Serving: 12 | Prep: 10mins | Ready in:

Ingredients

- 3 1/2 gallons peanut oil for frying

- 1 (10 pound) whole turkey, neck and giblets removed
- 1 tablespoon salt, or to taste
- 1 tablespoon ground black pepper, or to taste

Direction

- Pour oil on a turkey fryer or a big stockpot and heat it to 350 degrees F (175 degrees C). For safety purposes, please make sure that the fryer is in a safe area outdoors, away from buildings and other objects that could catch fire. For extra measures, have a fire extinguisher nearby. The turkey must be thawed completely. All extra skin trimmed, and neck hole is at least one inch wide. Using paper towels, pat the turkey completely dry. Rub pepper and salt generously outside and inside the bird. Position the turkey neck-side first on a drain basket. Very carefully and slowly, lower the drain basket into the oil until the turkey is completely submerged. Cook the turkey for approximately 35 minutes or 3 1/2 minutes per pound. Keep the oil temperature at 350 degrees (175 degrees C) so the bird will be cooked evenly.
- After carefully removing the drain basket from the oil, check inner temperature of the bird by inserting a meat thermometer into the thick area of thigh; it should be 180 degrees F (80 degrees C). Remove turkey from basket and drain excess oil with paper towels. Let rest for 15 minutes before carving.

Nutrition Information

- Calories: 9644 calories;
- Total Fat: 1053.2
- Sodium: 768
- Total Carbohydrate: 0.3
- Cholesterol: 224
- Protein: 76.7

209. Simple Mashed Sweet Potato Casserole

Serving: 4 | Prep: 10mins | Ready in:

Ingredients

- 2 cups mashed sweet potatoes
- 1/4 cup milk, or as needed
- 1/2 cup maple syrup
- 1/4 cup butter

Direction

- Heat the oven to 350°F (175°C). Coat a baking dish of 9x12 inches with oil.
- In a bowl, mash sweet potatoes with milk, putting in milk, a little at a time until potatoes get the consistency as desired. Spread sweet potatoes into the greased baking dish.
- In a saucepan, bring butter and maple syrup to a boil; then spread the boiling syrup mixture over sweet potatoes.
- Bake in the oven for 20-30 minutes, until sweet potatoes are hot and the topping starts to cook into a sticky caramel.

Nutrition Information

- Calories: 328 calories;
- Sodium: 159
- Total Carbohydrate: 54.1
- Cholesterol: 32
- Protein: 2.7
- Total Fat: 12.1

210. Simple Pumpkin Pie

Serving: 8 | Prep: 10mins | Ready in:

Ingredients

- 2 eggs
- 1 (16 ounce) can pumpkin puree
- 1 (14 ounce) can sweetened condensed milk

- 1 teaspoon pumpkin pie spice
- 1 (9 inch) unbaked pie crust

Direction

- Preheat an oven to 220°C or 425°F.
- In a big bowl, mix pumpkin pie spice, sweetened condensed milk, pumpkin puree and eggs and combine till incorporated.
- Into a pie dish 9-inch in size, fit the pie crust; put the pumpkin mixture into the crust.
- On a baking sheet, put the pie and allow to bake in the prepped oven for 15 minutes. Lower heat to 175°C or 350°F and bake for 35 to 40 minutes till filling is set.

Nutrition Information

- Calories: 309 calories;
- Protein: 7.5
- Total Fat: 13.2
- Sodium: 334
- Total Carbohydrate: 41.8
- Cholesterol: 63

211. Simple Roasted Butternut Squash

Serving: 4 | Prep: 15mins | Ready in:

Ingredients

- 1 butternut squash - peeled, seeded, and cut into 1-inch cubes
- 2 tablespoons olive oil
- 2 cloves garlic, minced
- salt and ground black pepper to taste

Direction

- Set the oven to 200°C or 400°F to preheat.
- In a big bowl, toss together butternut squash, garlic and olive oil. Season with black pepper and salt, then place coated squash on a baking sheet.
- In the preheated oven, roast for 25-30 minutes, until squash is browned slightly and softened.

Nutrition Information

- Calories: 177 calories;
- Total Carbohydrate: 30.3
- Cholesterol: 0
- Protein: 2.6
- Total Fat: 7
- Sodium: 11

212. Skinny Mashed Potatoes

Serving: 6 | Prep: 20mins | Ready in:

Ingredients

- 8 potatoes, peeled and diced
- 2 large onions, cut into chunks
- 2 cloves garlic, minced, or more to taste
- 1 cube vegetable bouillon, or more to taste
- water

Direction

- In a big pot, add bouillon cube, garlic, onions and potatoes, then add in enough water to cover halfway of the contents. Bring to a boil, then lower heat to moderately low and simmer for 15 minutes, until potatoes are tender.
- In the cooking liquid, mash potatoes until you get your wanted smoothness.

Nutrition Information

- Calories: 229 calories;
- Sodium: 22
- Total Carbohydrate: 52.1
- Cholesterol: 0
- Protein: 6.1
- Total Fat: 0.3

213. Special Turkey Gravy

Serving: 16 | Prep: 5mins | Ready in:

Ingredients

- 2 (1.2 ounce) packages turkey gravy mix
- 1/4 cup all-purpose flour
- 2 cups water
- 2 cups turkey pan drippings

Direction

- In a saucepan, put the flour and turkey gravy mix. Whisk in water gradually, followed by the turkey drippings until mixture is smooth. Over medium heat, bring to a boil, stirring often, turn to low heat and simmer the gravy for about 10 minutes until gravy thickens.

Nutrition Information

- Calories: 253 calories;
- Cholesterol: 27
- Protein: 0.6
- Total Fat: 25.8
- Sodium: 145
- Total Carbohydrate: 4.6

214. Spiced Maple Pumpkin Seeds

Serving: 8 | Prep: 10mins | Ready in:

Ingredients

- 1/4 cup butter
- 2 cups raw whole pumpkin seeds, washed and dried
- 1 teaspoon ground cinnamon
- 1/4 teaspoon ground nutmeg
- 2 tablespoons maple syrup

Direction

- Place parchment paper on a big baking tray or sheet and initially preheat the oven to 350°F (175°C).
- Melt the butter on a big skillet and cook the seeds over medium-low heat for 10 minutes. Continue stirring until the seeds become slightly brown. Put off the heat and drain to remove excess butter from the pan. Add in the maple syrup, cinnamon, and nutmeg and toss together until seeds are coated. Place the seeds on the baking sheet. Make sure to evenly spread it out before baking. Bake for 30 to 45 minutes until golden brown and crispy, mix it every 10 minutes.

Nutrition Information

- Calories: 136 calories;
- Total Carbohydrate: 12.2
- Cholesterol: 15
- Protein: 3
- Total Fat: 8.9
- Sodium: 44

215. Spiced Turkey Roast

Serving: 3 | Prep: | Ready in:

Ingredients

- 1 1/2 pounds boneless turkey roast
- 2 teaspoons olive oil
- 2 teaspoons ground cinnamon
- 2 teaspoons ground cloves
- 1 teaspoon ground allspice
- 1 tablespoon coarsely ground black pepper
- 1 cup cranberries
- 2 cups water
- 2 tablespoons orange juice
- 1 tablespoon cornstarch
- 2 tablespoons water

Direction

- Preheat an oven to 175°C or 350°F.
- In roasting pan, put the turkey, and massage with olive oil. Mix peppercorns, allspice, cloves and cinnamon; massage on the turkey.
- In oven, put the turkey and roast till juices run clear, approximately an hour.
- For the sauce, in a saucepan, mix 2 cups water and cranberries and boil. Reduce the heat and allow to cook till cranberries start to pop; put in orange juice. Mix 2 tablespoons water with arrowroot or cornstarch and put into sauce. Allow to cook till thick and serve on top of sliced turkey.

Nutrition Information

- Calories: 547 calories;
- Protein: 64.4
- Total Fat: 25.8
- Sodium: 161
- Total Carbohydrate: 11.9
- Cholesterol: 186

216. Spicy Chipotle Sweet Potato Soup

Serving: 8 | Prep: 20mins | Ready in:

Ingredients

- 2 tablespoons olive oil
- 1 large yellow onion, chopped
- 3 1/2 pounds sweet potatoes, peeled and cut into 2-inch chunks
- 4 1/2 cups vegetable broth, or as needed
- 1 (7 ounce) can chipotle peppers in adobo sauce, drained
- 1/2 cup heavy cream
- 2 limes, juiced
- salt to taste
- 1 cup sour cream
- 1/2 cup chopped fresh cilantro, or to taste

Direction

- Place a Dutch oven or a large saucepan on medium heat; heat olive oil; cook while stirring onion for 3-5 minutes in hot oil, till softened. Put in sweet potatoes; transfer in enough vegetable broth to cover the sweet potatoes; boil the mixture. Lower the heat; simmer with a partial cover for around 30 minutes, till the sweet potatoes are tender enough to easily pierce with a fork.
- Mix into the sweet potato mixture with the chipotle peppers.
- Using an immersion blender, blend the sweet potato mixture till the soup becomes smooth. Whisk lime juice and heavy cream into the soup till smooth and heated through; flavor with salt.
- Top each portion of the soup with a sprinkle of cilantro and 2 tablespoons of sour cream. Serve.

Nutrition Information

- Calories: 353 calories;
- Cholesterol: 33
- Protein: 5.2
- Total Fat: 15.7
- Sodium: 502
- Total Carbohydrate: 48.7

217. Spicy Portuguese Stuffing Balls

Serving: 12 | Prep: 25mins | Ready in:

Ingredients

- 3 loaves white bread, torn into pieces
- 1/2 cup water
- 1 large egg, beaten
- 1 1/2 cups lard
- 2 sweet onion (such as Vidalia®), chopped
- 1/2 cup chopped fresh parsley

- 1/3 cup cider vinegar
- 2 teaspoons red pepper flakes, or more to taste
- 1/2 teaspoon salt
- 1/2 teaspoon ground black pepper
- cooking spray

Direction

- Into one big bowl, put the bread. Add water on top of bread; put in egg. Use fists to force down the mixture, flipping as necessary, till bread is crumbled and moistened evenly.
- In big skillet, liquify lard on moderate heat. Put in parsley and onions; simmer for 10 minutes, till onions are soft. Turn heat to low. Mix in ground black pepper, salt, red pepper flakes and vinegar; simmer for 5 minutes, till flavors meld.
- On top of the bread mixture, add the onion mixture, flipping the bread while adding; stir till stuffing mixture is blended evenly.
- Preheat the oven to 165°C or 325°F. Use nonstick cooking spray to coat two baking sheets.
- Shape the stuffing mixture into three-inches rounds; put, 1 1/2-inch away, onto baking sheets.
- In the prepped oven, bake for 18 to 20 minutes, till golden brown.

Nutrition Information

- Calories: 558 calories;
- Total Fat: 29.9
- Sodium: 879
- Total Carbohydrate: 61.6
- Cholesterol: 40
- Protein: 9.8

218. Squash Pie

Serving: 8 | Prep: | Ready in:

Ingredients

- 1 recipe pastry for a 9 inch single crust pie
- 1 cup white sugar
- 1/8 teaspoon ground cinnamon
- 1/8 teaspoon ground nutmeg
- 1 pinch salt
- 1 tablespoon butter, melted
- 1/2 teaspoon ground ginger
- 2 cups hot milk
- 2 pounds butternut squash
- 3 eggs

Direction

- Start preheating the oven to 425°F (220°C). Add water to cover the squash cubes in a small saucepan. Bring to a boil and cook for 15 mins or until tender. Then drain, cool and mash. Measure out two cups mashed squash and place the leftover amount in refrigerator.
- Mix spices, salt, and sugar together. Blend in margarine or butter, eggs, squash and milk. Put the filling into the unbaked pie shell.
- Bake for 40 mins at 425°F (220°C), until a knife blade comes out clean when inserted in the middle.

Nutrition Information

- Calories: 320 calories;
- Total Fat: 12.1
- Sodium: 202
- Total Carbohydrate: 48.1
- Cholesterol: 78
- Protein: 6.9

219. Squash And Green Bean Saute Side Dish

Serving: 2 | Prep: 15mins | Ready in:

Ingredients

- 2 yellow squash, sliced
- 1 1/2 cups green beans

- 1 1/2 cups halved cherry tomatoes
- 2 tablespoons fresh lemon juice
- 1 tablespoon dried parsley
- 1/2 teaspoon ground coriander
- 1/8 teaspoon salt, or to taste
- 1/8 teaspoon ground black pepper, or to taste

Direction

- On medium heat, cook and stir green beans and squash for 2-3 minutes in a non-stick frying pan until slightly soft. Mix in black pepper, tomatoes, salt, lemon juice, coriander, and parsley. Cook and stir for 5-10 minutes until the tomatoes are soft.

Nutrition Information

- Calories: 89 calories;
- Total Fat: 0.9
- Sodium: 168
- Total Carbohydrate: 19.6
- Cholesterol: 0
- Protein: 5.1

220. Stuffed Delicata Squash

Serving: 2 | Prep: 10mins | Ready in:

Ingredients

- 1 delicata squash, halved lengthwise and seeded
- 2 teaspoons olive oil, divided, or as needed
- 2 apples - peeled, cored and diced
- 1/4 cup diced onion
- 1 clove garlic, minced
- 1/2 teaspoon finely chopped fresh rosemary
- 1 pinch ground cinnamon, or to taste
- salt and ground black pepper to taste
- 2 slices bacon
- 2 tablespoons goat cheese

Direction

- Set an oven to preheat to 200°C (400°F).
- Brush about 1 tsp. of olive oil inside the surface of delicata squash halves, then put it on a baking tray.
- Let it bake in the preheated oven for about 30 minutes, until it becomes tender once pierced using a fork.
- In a frying pan, heat the leftover 1 tsp. of olive oil on medium heat and cook and stir the onion and apples for about 5 minutes, until the onion becomes translucent. Stir cinnamon, rosemary and garlic into the apple mixture and sprinkle pepper and salt to season. Lower the heat to low and keep on cooking for about 5 minutes, stirring from time to time, until the apples become tender.
- In a frying pan, put the bacon and let it cook for about 8 minutes on medium-high heat, flipping from time to time, until it becomes crisp. Drain the slices of bacon on paper towels.
- Fill apple mixture on delicata halves. Crumble the goat cheese and bacon on top of the apple mixture.

Nutrition Information

- Calories: 282 calories;
- Protein: 6.5
- Total Fat: 11.2
- Sodium: 309
- Total Carbohydrate: 44.5
- Cholesterol: 15

221. Stuffed Turkey London Broil

Serving: 8 | Prep: 15mins | Ready in:

Ingredients

- 1 (2 pound) skinless, boneless turkey breast half

- 1 (10 ounce) package frozen chopped spinach, thawed, drained and squeezed dry
- 2 cups cooked brown rice
- 2 tablespoons cream cheese, or as needed
- 2 tablespoons toasted pine nuts, or to taste
- 1 pinch ground allspice, or to taste
- 1 pinch salt and ground black pepper to taste
- 2 tablespoons butter, cut into thin slices

Direction

- Preheat oven to 165°C/325°F. Prepare a 9 x 13-inch baking dish coated with grease.
- On the thick side of the turkey breast, make a deep pocket by slicing horizontally one deep cut using a sharp knife.
- Combine black pepper, salt, allspice, pine nuts, cream cheese, brown rice, and spinach; mix until combined thoroughly. Add a bit more cream cheese as needed if the stuffing does not hold together.
- On the baking dish, stuff the pockets of the turkey breast with the rice mixture and close the turkey breast with skewers. Pat thin dabs of butter on top of the turkey. Use aluminum foil to wrap and cover the baking dish.
- Bake for 1 hour, until the stuffing is heated and the turkey is not pink anymore. Remove from the oven, unwrap aluminum foil, and return turkey to the oven and bake for 45 more minutes, until browned thoroughly. Occasionally baste the turkey with the juices on the pan. Pierce an instant-read thermometer in the stuffing of the thickest part of the breast, it should read 75°C/165°F. Slice turkey across the grain. Serve.

Nutrition Information

- Calories: 249 calories;
- Total Carbohydrate: 13.5
- Cholesterol: 93
- Protein: 32.9
- Total Fat: 6.6
- Sodium: 109

222. Summer Squash And Onion Cheesy Casserole

Serving: 8 | Prep: 15mins | Ready in:

Ingredients

- 1 1/2 tablespoons butter, divided
- 3 summer squash, trimmed and cut into bite-size pieces
- 3 zucchini, trimmed and cut into bite-size pieces
- salt and ground black pepper to taste
- 3 onions, chopped
- 1 pound shredded sharp white Cheddar cheese
- 1/2 pound shredded Cheddar cheese
- 3 tablespoons sweetened condensed milk, divided

Direction

- Preheat oven to 175 degrees C/350 degrees F. grease 1/2 tbsp. butter on 9x9-in. baking dish.
- In a big cast-iron skillet, melt remaining 1 tbsp. butter on medium heat. Cook zucchini and summer squash for 10-15 minutes, stirring often, until squash pieces start to brown. Sprinkle black pepper and salt. Spread on the bottom of prepped baking dish. Sprinkle with about 1/3 chopped onions.
- In a bowl, thoroughly mix yellow and white cheddar cheese until combined. Sprinkle about 1/2 cup cheese mixture on onions. Drizzle 1 tbsp. sweetened condensed milk. Repeat cheese, onion, and the condensed milk sprinkling process two more times. Top with leftover cheese mixture.
- Bake in preheated oven for 30 minutes until onions are tender and casserole is golden brown.

Nutrition Information

- Calories: 438 calories;

- Total Fat: 31.3
- Sodium: 562
- Total Carbohydrate: 16.8
- Cholesterol: 97
- Protein: 24.1

223. Sweet Corn Casserole

Serving: 6 | Prep: 10mins | Ready in:

Ingredients

- 1 (15.25 ounce) can whole kernel corn, drained
- 1 (15 ounce) can cream-style corn
- 1 cup sugar
- 1 egg
- 1/4 cup butter, melted and divided
- 2 sleeves buttery round crackers (such as Ritz®), crushed and divided

Direction

- Preheat oven to 325° F (165° C).
- In a casserole dish, stir about 3/4 of the melted butter, egg, sugar, cream-style corn, and whole kernel corn together. Fold approximately 1/2 of the crushed crackers to mixture of corn. Scatter the rest of crushed crackers on top of the mixture then sprinkle with the leftover butter.
- In the preheated oven, bake for 25 – 30 minutes till beginning to brown.

Nutrition Information

- Calories: 516 calories;
- Total Carbohydrate: 83.4
- Cholesterol: 48
- Protein: 6.5
- Total Fat: 19.9
- Sodium: 848

224. Sweet Onion Broccoli Cornbread

Serving: 8 | Prep: 15mins | Ready in:

Ingredients

- 1 large sweet onion (such as Vidalia®), finely chopped
- 1 (10 ounce) package frozen chopped broccoli, thawed
- 3/4 cup cottage cheese
- 4 beaten eggs
- 1 (7.5 ounce) package corn bread mix (such as Jiffy®)
- 1 teaspoon salt
- 1/2 cup margarine, melted

Direction

- Preheat the oven to 220 °C or 425 °F. Oil a metal 9x9-inch baking pan.
- Combine the margarine, corn bread mix, eggs, cottage cheese, broccoli and sweet onion in a bowl. Into the prepared baking pan, spoon the mixture.
- In the prepared oven, bake for 45 minutes till casserole has risen and top is browned.

Nutrition Information

- Calories: 277 calories;
- Sodium: 981
- Total Carbohydrate: 22.1
- Cholesterol: 97
- Protein: 9.2
- Total Fat: 17.4

225. Sweet Potato Cranberry Bake

Serving: 10 | Prep: 10mins | Ready in:

Ingredients

- 1 (12 ounce) package whole cranberries
- 1 small unpeeled orange, sliced
- 1 1/3 cups white sugar
- 1/2 cup pecan pieces
- 1/4 cup orange juice
- 3/4 teaspoon ground cinnamon
- 1/4 teaspoon ground nutmeg
- 1/8 teaspoon ground mace
- 1 (40 ounce) can cut yams, drained

Direction

- Preheat an oven to 190°C/375°F.
- Mix mace, nutmeg, cinnamon, orange juice, pecans, sugar, orange slices and cranberries in a 2-qt. baking dish.
- In preheated oven, bake for 30 minutes till cranberries soften. Mix yams into cranberry mixture; bake for 15 minutes more till heated through.

Nutrition Information

- Calories: 218 calories;
- Protein: 1.4
- Total Fat: 4.5
- Sodium: 25
- Total Carbohydrate: 45.3
- Cholesterol: 0

226. Sweet Potato Eggnog Casserole

Serving: 8 | Prep: 15mins | Ready in:

Ingredients

- 2 (15 ounce) cans sweet potatoes, mashed
- 1 cup eggnog
- 2 tablespoons butter, melted
- 3/4 cup white sugar
- 1/2 teaspoon salt
- 1/2 teaspoon ground ginger
- 1/4 teaspoon ground cloves
- 2 tablespoons grated orange zest
- 1/2 cup chopped pecans

Direction

- Preheat the oven to 190°C/375°F.
- Mix pecans, orange zest, clove, ginger, salt, sugar, butter, eggnog and sweet potatoes in a big bowl; put in a 2-qt. baking dish.
- In the preheated oven, bake for 40 minutes till golden on top and heated through.

Nutrition Information

- Calories: 297 calories;
- Total Fat: 10.4
- Sodium: 263
- Total Carbohydrate: 49.1
- Cholesterol: 26
- Protein: 4

227. Sweet Potato Sage Balls

Serving: 6 | Prep: 10mins | Ready in:

Ingredients

- cooking spray
- 1/2 cup finely diced onion
- 2 cloves chopped garlic
- 1 cup old-fashioned rolled oats
- 3/4 cup mashed sweet potatoes
- 1 egg
- 1 1/2 teaspoons dried sage
- 1/4 teaspoon ground black pepper

Direction

- Over medium heat, heat a small skillet and coat in cooking spray. In the skillet, cook and mix garlic and onion for approximately 5 minutes till clear.
- Over medium heat, heat a griddle and coat in cooking spray.

- In a bowl, mix together black pepper, sage, egg, sweet potatoes and oats; put the onion mixture. Form the mixture into golf-size balls and slightly flatten.
- On the prepped griddle, let sweet potato balls cook for about 4 minutes each side till browned.

Nutrition Information

- Calories: 103 calories;
- Total Fat: 1.9
- Sodium: 37
- Total Carbohydrate: 18.3
- Cholesterol: 31
- Protein: 3.7

228. Tequila And Orange Cranberry Sauce

Serving: 16 | Prep: 5mins | Ready in:

Ingredients

- 1/4 cup orange juice
- 1 (1.5 fluid ounce) jigger tequila
- 2 teaspoons grated orange zest
- 1 1/2 pounds fresh cranberries
- 1 3/4 cups white sugar
- 1 pinch salt

Direction

- In a saucepan, bring orange zest, tequila and orange juice to a boil on moderate heat. Put in salt, sugar and cranberries then simmer about 25 minutes until creates a jam-like sauce.
- Use an immersion blender to blend sauce for a smoother consistency. Allow to cool and sauce will keep on thickening naturally.

Nutrition Information

- Calories: 112 calories;
- Total Fat: 0.1
- Sodium: 11
- Total Carbohydrate: 27.5
- Cholesterol: 0
- Protein: 0.2

229. Thanksgiving Any Day Rollups

Serving: 3 | Prep: 15mins | Ready in:

Ingredients

- 1 (8 ounce) package reduced-fat cream cheese
- 1/2 (8 ounce) package shredded Cheddar cheese
- 12 meatless turkey-flavored deli slices (such as Tofurky®), chopped
- 1/3 cup dried cranberries
- 1/4 cup pecans
- 1 celery stick, chopped
- 2 green onions, chopped
- 1 tablespoon chopped fresh chives
- salt and ground black pepper to taste
- 3 large flour tortillas

Direction

- In food processor, combine Cheddar cheese and cream cheese. Then process until they are blended. Put in black pepper, salt, chives, green onions, celery, pecans, cranberries and meatless turkey slices. Process until they become smooth.
- Spread each tortilla with the cream cheese mixture, then roll up. Enjoy immediately or place in the refrigerator until serving time.

Nutrition Information

- Calories: 773 calories;
- Total Fat: 39.2
- Sodium: 1196
- Total Carbohydrate: 69.5

- Cholesterol: 82
- Protein: 36.9

230. Thanksgiving Bacon Stuffing

Serving: 12 | Prep: 15mins | Ready in:

Ingredients

- 1 pound bacon, cut into 1/2-inch pieces
- 1/2 cup butter
- 1 cup finely chopped onion
- 1 cup chopped celery
- 2 tablespoons poultry seasoning (such as Bell's®)
- 2 loaves day-old white bread, torn into small pieces
- 2 eggs, beaten

Direction

- Preheat an oven to 200°C/400°F.
- In a big skillet, cook bacon on medium high heat till cooked through yet slightly soft, about 5-10 minutes. On paper towels, drain bacon slices; leaving bacon drippings in skillet.
- Melt butter in another skillet on medium high heat; sauté celery and onion for 5 minutes till soft. Mix poultry seasoning and bacon into the onion mixture.
- Mix together bread pieces and onion-bacon mixture in a big bowl; fold in eggs. Put bread mixture in muffin cups.
- In the preheated oven, bake for 25 minutes till tops are crispy.

Nutrition Information

- Calories: 357 calories;
- Protein: 11.8
- Total Fat: 16.3
- Sodium: 877
- Total Carbohydrate: 40.5

- Cholesterol: 65

231. Thanksgiving Cookies

Serving: 32 | Prep: 30mins | Ready in:

Ingredients

- 3 cups quick cooking oats
- 1 (14 ounce) can solid-pack pumpkin puree
- 1 (12 ounce) bag semisweet chocolate chips
- 1 3/4 cups all-purpose flour
- 1 cup butter, softened
- 1/2 cup white sugar
- 1 egg

Direction

- Set the oven to 190°C or 375°F to preheat.
- In a bowl, combine together egg, sugar, butter, flour, chocolate chips, pumpkin and oats until dough becomes thick and well combined. Form dough into 2 to 3-in. patties, then arrange on a baking sheet.
- In the preheated oven, bake for about 15-20 minutes, until patties are cooked through.

Nutrition Information

- Calories: 173 calories;
- Sodium: 75
- Total Carbohydrate: 21.1
- Cholesterol: 21
- Protein: 2.5
- Total Fat: 9.7

232. Thanksgiving Quesadilla

Serving: 6 | Prep: 10mins | Ready in:

Ingredients

- 2 flour tortillas
- 1/2 cup shredded Cheddar cheese
- 1/4 pound shredded cooked turkey meat
- 2 tablespoons cranberry sauce
- 1/2 jalapeno pepper, seeded and minced
- 1 green onion, sliced
- 2 tablespoons chopped fresh cilantro, or to taste

Direction

- Heat a skillet over medium heat. In the skillet, put 1 tortilla and put 1/2 of the Cheddar cheese, turkey, cranberry sauce, jalapeno pepper, green onion and the remaining Cheddar cheese on top of the tortilla in order. Top with the remaining tortilla.
- Cook until the tortilla has a golden-brown color and the cheese melts, approximately 2-4 minutes on each side.

Nutrition Information

- Calories: 141 calories;
- Cholesterol: 26
- Protein: 9.9
- Total Fat: 5.9
- Sodium: 165
- Total Carbohydrate: 11.6

233. Thanksgiving Spinach Salad

Serving: 4 | Prep: 10mins | Ready in:

Ingredients

- 3/4 cup sweetened dried cranberries, chopped
- 1 McIntosh apple - peeled, cored, and diced
- 1/2 small red onion, finely chopped
- 2 tablespoons lemon juice
- 2 teaspoons honey
- 1 teaspoon chili powder
- 1/2 teaspoon ground cinnamon
- 1 (6 ounce) bag baby spinach, torn into bite-sized pieces

Direction

- In a big bowl, mix together cinnamon, chili powder, honey, lemon juice, onion, apple and cranberries. Allow to rest for 20 minutes to let flavors blend together. Put in spinach and toss to coat.

Nutrition Information

- Calories: 115 calories;
- Sodium: 41
- Total Carbohydrate: 30
- Cholesterol: 0
- Protein: 1.5
- Total Fat: 0.3

234. The Best Banana Pudding

Serving: 20 | Prep: 25mins | Ready in:

Ingredients

- 1 (5 ounce) package instant vanilla pudding mix
- 2 cups cold milk
- 1 (14 ounce) can sweetened condensed milk
- 1 tablespoon vanilla extract
- 1 (12 ounce) container frozen whipped topping, thawed
- 1 (16 ounce) package vanilla wafers
- 14 bananas, sliced

Direction

- Beat milk and pudding mix for 2 minutes in a big mixing bowl; blend in condensed milk till smooth. Mix in vanilla; fold in whipped topping. In a glass serving bowl, layer pudding mixture, bananas and wafers; chill till serving.

Nutrition Information

- Calories: 329 calories;
- Protein: 4.2
- Total Fat: 9.6
- Sodium: 205
- Total Carbohydrate: 56.9
- Cholesterol: 9

235. Thyme Roasted Sweet Potatoes

Serving: 4 | Prep: 15mins | Ready in:

Ingredients

- 4 sweet potatoes, peeled and cut into 1 1/2-inch thick rounds
- 1/3 cup fresh thyme leaves
- 3 tablespoons olive oil
- 4 large garlic cloves, minced
- 1/2 teaspoon kosher salt
- 1/2 teaspoon red pepper flakes

Direction

- Preheat an oven to 230°C/450°F.
- Mix red pepper flakes, salt, garlic, olive oil, thyme and sweet potatoes till evenly coated in a bowl. Put coated sweet potato slices on a 9x13-in. baking dish/rimmed baking sheet, in single layer.
- Put baking sheet on the preheated oven's top rack; roast for 40 minutes till sweet potatoes are slightly brown and tender.

Nutrition Information

- Calories: 297 calories;
- Cholesterol: 0
- Protein: 4.1
- Total Fat: 10.4
- Sodium: 366
- Total Carbohydrate: 48.3

236. Turkey Divan

Serving: 6 | Prep: 10mins | Ready in:

Ingredients

- 2 (10 ounce) packages frozen broccoli spears
- 1/4 cup margarine
- 6 tablespoons all-purpose flour
- salt and ground black pepper to taste
- 2 cups chicken broth
- 1/2 cup heavy whipping cream
- 3 tablespoons white wine
- 3 cups cooked turkey breast, sliced
- 1/4 cup shredded Monterey Jack cheese

Direction

- In a saucepan, put broccoli and 4 cups of water. Boil; lower the heat; simmer with a cover for 5-8 minutes, or till tender. Drain.
- Set the oven at 350°F (175°C) and start preheating.
- In a saucepan over medium heat, melt margarine; mix in pepper, salt and flour, stir properly. Pour in chicken broth; cook while stirring for around 10 minutes, or till the sauce bubbles and thickens. Pour in wine and cream; stir till well combined.
- On the bottom of a 7x12-in. baking sheet, place broccoli. Spread half of the sauce over broccoli. Arrange sliced turkey on top. In the saucepan, mix Monterey Jack cheese into the remaining sauce. Transfer the cheese sauce over the turkey.
- Bake in the preheated oven for around 20 minutes, or till bubbly. Keep broiling for around 5 minutes, or till the cheese sauce turns golden.

Nutrition Information

- Calories: 331 calories;
- Total Fat: 20.1
- Sodium: 218
- Total Carbohydrate: 11.4
- Cholesterol: 85
- Protein: 25.6

237. Turkey Paupiettes With Apple Maple Stuffing

Serving: 4 | Prep: 20mins | Ready in:

Ingredients

- 2 tablespoons extra virgin olive oil, divided
- 2 links apple maple chicken sausage, casings removed
- 1 small onion, diced
- 2 cloves garlic, minced
- 1 cup crusty bread cubes
- 4 teaspoons finely chopped fresh parsley
- 1/2 tablespoon finely chopped fresh sage
- 1 (1 1/2-pound) skinless, boneless turkey breast half, halved lengthwise and pounded to 1/2-inch thickness
- salt and ground black pepper to taste
- 1 cup turkey stock

Direction

- Put 1 tbsp. of olive oil in a nonstick skillet and heat it over medium-high heat. Stir in sausage and cook for 5-10 minutes, breaking it using the wooden spoon until crumbly and browned. Place the cooked sausage into a large bowl. Set the skillet back into the heat.
- Cook and stir garlic and onion into the hot skillet for 3-4 minutes until fragrant and softened. Once cooked, place them into the bowl with sausage.
- In a food processor, blend the bread cubes until finely ground. Pour the bread crumbs, sage, and parsley into the sausage mixture. Mix well until the stuffing is combined.
- Season the turkey breasts with salt and pepper. Spoon half of the stuffing mixture onto each of the breasts. Roll the turkey breasts around the stuffing, tucking the sides inside as you roll. Secure the rolls with twine. Season each of the rolls with salt and pepper.
- Set the oven to 350°F (175°C) for preheating.
- Put leftover 1 tbsp. of olive oil in a large oven-proof skillet and heat it over medium-high heat. Cook the turkey rolls in hot oil for 3-5 minutes per side until golden brown on every side.
- Pour the turkey stock into the skillet. Let the mixture boil while scraping off any browned bits at the bottom of the pan using the wooden spoon. Place the skillet into the oven.
- Let them cook inside the preheated oven for 10-12 minutes until the juices run clear and the rolls are no longer pink in the middle. An inserted instant-read thermometer into the center registers at least 165°F (74°C). Get the rolls from the oven and allow them to rest for 5 minutes. Cut the rolls into 1-inch slices.

Nutrition Information

- Calories: 374 calories;
- Total Fat: 13.7
- Sodium: 526
- Total Carbohydrate: 7.7
- Cholesterol: 175
- Protein: 52.1

238. Turkey Scallopini And Squash Ravioli With Cranberry Brown Butter

Serving: 8 | Prep: 10mins | Ready in:

Ingredients

- 8 (4 ounce) portions boneless turkey breast
- 1/4 cup extra-virgin olive oil
- 1/4 cup all-purpose flour

- 2 eggs, beaten
- 2 cups Progresso® plain Panko crispy bread crumbs
- 8 tablespoons unsalted butter
- 1 (18 ounce) package frozen squash ravioli
- 1/4 cup chopped fresh sage
- 1 1/2 cups fresh cranberries
- 3 tablespoons dark molasses
- 1/4 cup balsamic vinegar
- 1 cup Progresso® chicken broth or reduced-sodium chicken broth
- Salt and pepper

Direction

- In a big pot, boil 4 quarts lightly salted water.
- Using a meat mallet, pound turkey breast pieces between two sheets of plastic wrap to an even quarter-inch thickness. Back of a frying pan can be used if meat mallet is not available. This can be done a day in advance and keep in the plastic wrap, folded on top of each other. Or a butcher can cut and pound the turkey on your behalf.
- In a big sauté pan, heat olive oil over medium-high heat. Coat the turkey pieces lightly with flour, and shake off the excess; dunk in beaten eggs and then roll in bread crumbs. Once oil is bubbling and hot, put turkey pieces. Avoid crowding the pan. Let brown for 2 to 3 minutes, then flip to cook the other side, for another 30 seconds to a minute. The turkey will cook really quickly and will dry out if overcooked. Once done, take off to a baking sheet or platter and retain warmth. Avoid washing the sauté pan.
- For the sauce, put butter to sauté pan over medium-high heat. At the same time, into the boiling water, drop the ravioli. Once butter starts to become light brown, put fresh sage. Mix for several seconds; then put cranberries, and sauté till skins start to burst. Put broth, balsamic vinegar and molasses, scraping base of the pan to get all the flavor of the turkey. Allow to simmer till cranberries are tender and the sauce coats the back of a spoon for about 12 to 15 minutes. Season with salt and pepper to taste. Ensure to taste sauce for seasoning prior to pouring it on top of the turkey.
- Try ravioli doneness in about 3 minutes, press edges of dough; it should be soft. Let it drain. Arrange quarter of the raviolis per serving on hot plates and layer 1 piece of turkey on top of the ravioli. Spoon sauce on tops.

Nutrition Information

- Calories: 724 calories;
- Sodium: 1451
- Total Carbohydrate: 69.1
- Cholesterol: 135
- Protein: 34.3
- Total Fat: 34.1

239. Turkey Tenderloins

Serving: 4 | Prep: | Ready in:

Ingredients

- 1 pound turkey tenderloins
- 3 tablespoons soy sauce
- 1 tablespoon Dijon-style prepared mustard
- 2 teaspoons dried rosemary, crushed

Direction

- In a sealable plastic bag, put turkey tenderloins and put aside.
- Mix the rosemary, mustard and soy sauce in a small bowl. Put on top of turkey, close the bag and coat by shaking. Refrigerate to marinate for 1 to 4 hours, shaking one or two times.
- Preheat the oven on broiler setting. Take turkey out of the marinade and put on rack in broiler pan. Broil 4 inches away from the heat source for 20 to 22 minutes, flipping once, till meat is cooked completely and juices run clear once pricked with a fork. Cut and serve together with Cranberry Chutney.

Nutrition Information

- Calories: 154 calories;
- Sodium: 825
- Total Carbohydrate: 2
- Cholesterol: 79
- Protein: 27.7
- Total Fat: 3.1

240. Turkey A La King

Serving: 4 | Prep: 10mins | Ready in:

Ingredients

- 2 tablespoons butter
- 3 fresh mushrooms, sliced
- 1 tablespoon all-purpose flour
- 1 cup chicken broth
- 1/2 cup heavy cream
- 1 cup chopped cooked turkey
- 1/3 cup frozen peas, thawed
- salt and pepper to taste

Direction

- Cook butter in a big skillet over moderately low heat till golden brown. Sauté the mushrooms till soft. Mix in flour till smooth. Gradually mix in chicken broth, and cook till thickened slightly. Mix in peas, turkey and cream. Turn the heat to low, and let cook till thickened. Add pepper and salt to season.

Nutrition Information

- Calories: 233 calories;
- Sodium: 92
- Total Carbohydrate: 4.5
- Cholesterol: 83
- Protein: 12.2
- Total Fat: 18.6

241. Two Ingredient Pumpkin Cake

Serving: 15 | Prep: 5mins | Ready in:

Ingredients

- 1 (18.25 ounce) package spice cake mix
- 1 (15 ounce) can pumpkin

Direction

- Preheat an oven to 175°C/350°F. Grease 9x13-in. baking pan generously.
- Mix canned pumpkin and spice cake mix till blended well in big bowl. Evenly spread in the prepared pan.
- In preheated oven, bake for 25-30 minutes till an inserted knife in middle exits cleanly. Cool; serve. You can keep in the fridge. This tastes better the following day.

Nutrition Information

- Calories: 157 calories;
- Total Fat: 4.3
- Sodium: 300
- Total Carbohydrate: 27.5
- Cholesterol: 0
- Protein: 2.4

242. Vintage Fresh Green Bean Casserole (circa 1956)

Serving: 12 | Prep: 15mins | Ready in:

Ingredients

- 4 pounds fresh green beans, trimmed and cut into 2-inch pieces
- 2 (10.75 ounce) cans cream of mushroom soup
- 1 pound sharp Cheddar cheese, grated
- 1 (6 ounce) can French-fried onions

Direction

- Set oven to 350°F (175°C) to preheat.
- Bring salted water in a large saucepan to boiling; cook green beans in boiling water for about 5 minutes until just tender partially. Drain off water.
- In a mixing bowl, combine cream of mushroom soup and green beans; scatter into a 9x13-inch baking dish. Sprinkle with Cheddar cheese and top with French-fries onions.
- Bake for about half an hour minutes in the preheated oven until cheese melts and has turned brown.

Nutrition Information

- Calories: 333 calories;
- Sodium: 692
- Total Carbohydrate: 20.7
- Cholesterol: 40
- Protein: 13
- Total Fat: 22.7

243. Warm Brie And Pear Tartlets

Serving: 24 | Prep: 15mins | Ready in:

Ingredients

- 24 mini phyllo tart shells
- 1/4 pound ripe Brie cheese, cut into 24 small chunks
- 1 ripe pear, cut into small dice
- 2 sprigs fresh thyme
- 2 tablespoons honey, or to taste

Direction

- Preheat oven to 200°C/400°F. Line a parchment paper onto a jelly roll pan.
- On the prepared pan, arrange the tart shells. Add a piece of Brie cheese to each tart shell. Sprinkle with a couple of thyme leaves and diced pear. Drizzle honey on top.
- Bake for 12 to 15 minutes in the preheated oven, or until the tarts are golden and the cheese has melted.

Nutrition Information

- Calories: 48 calories;
- Total Carbohydrate: 5
- Cholesterol: 5
- Protein: 1.5
- Total Fat: 2.3
- Sodium: 40

244. Wet Turkey Apple Brine

Serving: 1 | Prep: 15mins | Ready in:

Ingredients

- 2 gallons cold water
- 3 cups apple juice
- 1 cup brown sugar
- 1 cup kosher salt
- 1 orange, peeled
- 1/4 cup chopped fresh rosemary
- 2 tablespoons whole black peppercorns
- 1 1/2 tablespoons minced garlic
- 1 1/2 teaspoons whole allspice berries
- 1 1/2 teaspoons chopped crystallized ginger
- 5 bay leaves

Direction

- In stock pot, mix bay leaves, ginger, allspice, garlic, peppercorns, rosemary, orange peel, kosher salt, brown sugar, apple juice and water; let come to a slow boil. Turn off heat and let cool to room temperature.

Nutrition Information

- Calories: 1264 calories;

- Sodium: 91414
- Total Carbohydrate: 321.4
- Cholesterol: 0
- Protein: 3.2
- Total Fat: 1.9

245. White Chocolate Chip Pumpkin Cupcakes

Serving: 24 | Prep: 10mins | Ready in:

Ingredients

- 1 (16.25 ounce) package moist white cake mix (such as Betty Crocker® SuperMoist®)
- 1 1/4 cups water
- 1/3 cup vegetable oil
- 3 egg whites
- 1 (15 ounce) can pumpkin puree
- 1 teaspoon pumpkin pie spice
- 1 (8 ounce) package miniature white chocolate chips (such as Nestle® Toll House®)
- 1 (16 ounce) container cream cheese frosting

Direction

- Preheat the oven to 175°C or 350°F. Grease 2 dozen muffin cups or line using paper liners.
- In bowl, whip egg whites, oil, water and cake mix on low with electric mixer for 30 seconds. Raise the speed to moderate and whip till batter becomes smooth, for an additional of 2 minutes. Mix pumpkin pie spice and pumpkin puree in batter; fold white chocolate chips in. Scoop the batter to prepped muffin cups, keeping roughly half-inch headspace. Cupcakes rise quite a bit.
- In prepped oven, bake for 20 to 25 minutes, till an inserted toothpick in the middle of one cupcake gets out clean. Turn cupcakes onto wire rack to fully cool. Use cream cheese frosting to frost the cupcakes.

Nutrition Information

- Calories: 255 calories;
- Total Fat: 13
- Sodium: 233
- Total Carbohydrate: 33.1
- Cholesterol: 2
- Protein: 2.2

246. White Sauce

Serving: 8 | Prep: 5mins | Ready in:

Ingredients

- 2 tablespoons butter
- 2 tablespoons all-purpose flour
- 1 cup milk

Direction

- In a small saucepan, heat butter over medium heat until melted. Add flour and mix until the flour and butter thoroughly blend. Add milk, whisking continually while it gets thick. Pour in additional milk depending on the consistency you want.

Nutrition Information

- Calories: 48 calories;
- Total Fat: 3.5
- Sodium: 33
- Total Carbohydrate: 2.9
- Cholesterol: 10
- Protein: 1.2

247. White Wine Turkey Gravy

Serving: 18 | Prep: 10mins | Ready in:

Ingredients

- 5 cups turkey drippings

- 1 cup dry white wine
- 1 tablespoon dried rosemary
- 1 tablespoon ground black pepper, or to taste
- 3 tablespoons cornstarch, or as needed
- salt to taste

Direction

- Use a fine mesh sieve to strain the turkey drippings into a big saucepan. Reserve 1 cup of drippings in a bowl. In a saucepan with the drippings, stir black pepper, rosemary and white wine and over medium low heat, bring to a simmer. For about 20 minutes, simmer to blend the flavors and to cook off the alcohol. Whisk cornstarch in the bowl with the drippings and in the hot gravy, whisk the cornstarch mixture in. For about 3 minutes, allow the gravy to simmer until thickened. Stir salt in to taste. Before serving, strain out any big pieces of rosemary.

Nutrition Information

- Calories: 530 calories;
- Sodium: 1
- Total Carbohydrate: 1.9
- Cholesterol: 58
- Protein: 0.1
- Total Fat: 56.9

---

248. Yellow Squash Casserole

Serving: 10 | Prep: 20mins | Ready in:

Ingredients

- 4 cups sliced yellow squash
- 1/2 cup chopped onion
- 35 buttery round crackers, crushed
- 1 cup shredded Cheddar cheese
- 2 eggs, beaten
- 3/4 cup milk
- 1/4 cup butter, melted
- 1 teaspoon salt
- ground black pepper to taste
- 2 tablespoons butter

Direction

- Preheat an oven to 200°C/400°F.
- Put onion and squash in big skillet on medium heat; put small amount of water in. Cover; cook for 5 minutes till squash is tender. Drain well; put in big bowl.
- Mix cheese and cracker crumbs in medium bowl. Mix 1/2 cracker mixture into onions and cooked squash. Mix milk and eggs in small bowl; add into squash mixture. Mix 1/4 cup melted butter in; season with pepper and salt. Spread in 9x13-in. baking dish. Sprinkle leftover cracker mixture; dot with 2 tbsp. butter.
- In preheated oven, bake till lightly browned for 25 minutes.

Nutrition Information

- Calories: 196 calories;
- Total Carbohydrate: 10.3
- Cholesterol: 69
- Protein: 6.1
- Total Fat: 14.8
- Sodium: 463

---

249. Zena's Cranberry Apple Cider Punch

Serving: 1 | Prep: 5mins | Ready in:

Ingredients

- ice cubes
- 1 1/2 fluid ounces spiced rum
- 1 fluid ounce apple cider
- 1/2 fluid ounce cranberry juice

Direction

- Add ice to file a glass. Pour cranberry juice, apple cider and spiced rum over the ice then stir.

Nutrition Information

- Calories: 120 calories;
- Total Carbohydrate: 6
- Cholesterol: 0
- Protein: 0
- Total Fat: 0
- Sodium: 5

- Bake for 15 mins in prepared oven, until cheese is bubbly.

Nutrition Information

- Calories: 537 calories;
- Total Fat: 28.9
- Sodium: 852
- Total Carbohydrate: 44.9
- Cholesterol: 67
- Protein: 25.6

250. Zucchilattas

Serving: 10 | Prep: 15mins | Ready in:

Ingredients

- 2 tablespoons butter
- 1 1/2 pounds sliced zucchini
- 1 pound mushrooms, sliced
- 1 onion, sliced
- 1 1/2 pounds tomatoes, chopped
- salt and pepper to taste
- 1 1/2 pounds Monterey Jack cheese, shredded
- 10 (10 inch) flour tortillas

Direction

- Start preheating the oven to 350°F (175°C). Lightly grease a 9x13-in. baking dish with oil.
- In a large skillet, melt butter over medium heat. Mix pepper, salt, tomatoes, onion, mushrooms and zucchini together. Then put them into skillet. Cook while stirring until vegetables become soft.
- Warm tortillas in prepared oven until soft, about 2 to 3 mins. Stuff Monterey Jack cheese and zucchini mixture into warmed tortillas, saving some both for toppings. Then roll filled tortillas then place in baking dish, seam side facing down. Add remaining zucchini mixture to cover. Place the remaining cheese on top.

Index

A

Almond 3,12

Apple 3,4,5,6,7,8,10,13,16,23,24,26,30,34,36,47,53,86,92,93,111,114,116

Asparagus 3,9

B

Bacon 3,5,10,11,12,20,86,108

Baking 92

Banana 3,5,14,109

Beans 3,4,5,12,20,23,39,64,97

Blackberry 3,18

Bread 3,4,5,15,53,91

Brie 3,5,19,114

Broccoli 3,5,20,25,105

Brussels sprouts 21,51,52,67,86,93

Butter 3,4,5,13,22,23,49,65,66,76,86,92,93,97,99,111

C

Cake 3,4,5,28,31,81,82,88,113

Caramel 4,5,70,86

Carrot 3,4,18,34,51,59,64,66

Cauliflower 4,50,62

Chard 93

Cheddar 6,17,20,23,26,41,44,71,79,95,96,104,107,109,113,114,116

Cheese 3,4,18,19,20,31,32,43

Chicken 3,27

Chipotle 4,5,81,101

Chocolate 3,5,28,35,91,115

Chutney 112

Cider 3,5,6,116

Cinnamon 3,4,34,50,65,68

Cocktail 5,82,96

Coffee 4,47

Cranberry 3,4,5,30,31,32,38,40,41,48,50,57,60,63,65,73,76,78,86,87,105,107,111,112,116

Cream 3,4,7,31,32,33,42,53,72

Crumble 4,55,103

Curd 4,63

D

Dijon mustard 29,35,67

E

Egg 3,4,5,29,35,36,71,106

F

Fat 6,7,8,9,10,11,12,13,14,15,16,17,18,19,20,21,22,23,24,25,26,27,28,29,30,31,32,33,34,35,36,37,38,39,40,41,42,43,44,45,46,47,48,49,50,51,52,53,54,55,56,57,58,59,60,61,62,63,64,65,66,67,68,69,70,71,72,73,74,75,76,77,78,79,80,81,82,83,84,85,86,87,88,89,90,91,92,93,94,95,96,97,98,99,100,101,102,103,104,105,106,107,108,109,110,111,112,113,114,115,116,117

Feta 3,11

G

Garlic 3,4,12,23,49,50

Gin 4,5,50,57,65,68,87

Gratin 3,4,21,72,79

Gravy 3,4,5,30,39,46,52,58,72,77,78,92,100,115

H

Ham 3,4,26,65

Honey 4,59,76

J

Jam 3,16

Jus 74

K

Kale 3,4,13,63

L

Lemon 4,64

M

Milk 5,90

Muffins 3,14

Mushroom 4,5,72,85

Mustard 71

N

Nut 3,4,5,6,7,8,9,10,11,12,13,14,15,16,17,18,19,20,21,22,23,24,25,26,27,28,29,30,31,32,33,34,35,36,37,38,39,40,41,42,43,44,45,46,47,48,49,50,51,52,53,54,55,56,57,58,59,60,61,62,63,64,65,66,67,68,69,70,71,72,73,74,75,76,77,78,79,80,81,82,83,84,85,86,87,88,89,90,91,92,93,94,95,96,97,98,99,100,101,102,103,104,105,106,107,108,109,110,111,112,113,114,115,116,117

O

Oatmeal 3,7,30

Oil 13,39,58,80,89,96,105

Onion 5,93,104,105

Orange 3,5,38,41,107

Oyster 4,5,50,96

P

Pancakes 4,42,79

Parmesan 4,21,33,39,41,46,50,63,72,73,75,76

Parsley 5,94

Parsnip 4,79

Pasta 4,81

Pear 3,4,5,18,59,76,91,114

Pecan 3,4,16,22,31,68,69,76,77

Peel 35,93

Pepper 4,5,64,94

Pie 3,4,5,16,26,27,38,40,43,49,63,68,69,77,82,83,86,90,98,102,104

Pineapple 4,78

Pistachio 3,4,19,62

Pizza 3,19

Pomegranate 4,78

Pork 3,10

Port 5,101

Potato 3,4,5,6,15,24,26,27,34,45,56,60,68,69,72,74,79,80,95,97,98,99,101,105,106,110

Poultry 61

Pulse 55,92,95

Pumpkin 3,4,5,8,9,28,33,37,38,42,43,47,49,55,81,82,83,84,85,88,89,90,92,96,98,100,113,115

Q

Quinoa 5,91

R

Raisins 5,93

Raspberry 3,38

Rice 3,5,25,85,88

Rosemary 5,95

S

Sage 4,5,56,95,106

Salad 3,4,5,8,10,17,21,29,62,67,73,74,109

Salt 112

Sausage 3,4,5,7,43,52,90,96

Savory 3,29

Scallop 5,111

Seasoning 20,61

Seeds 5,95,100

Soup 3,5,22,34,83,84,101

Spinach 3,5,11,93,95,109

Squash 3,4,5,10,13,22,44,49,66,93,95,97,99,102,103,104,111,116

Stuffing 3,4,5,7,13,15,25,45,47,53,90,91,101,108,111

Sugar 3,20

T

Tequila 5,107

Thyme 5,110

Tofu 107

Turkey 3,4,5,11,17,27,29,32,40,44,46,56,58,61,67,68,70,74,77,88,92,94,97,100,103,110,111,112,113,114,115

V

Vegan 3,35

Vegetarian 4,62

W

Waffles 4,79

Walnut 3,5,8,93

Wine 3,4,5,29,59,91,115

Worcestershire sauce 50,51,70

Y

Yam 4,70

Yeast 5,89

Conclusion

Thank you again for downloading this book!

I hope you enjoyed reading about my book!

If you enjoyed this book, please take the time to share your thoughts and post a review on Amazon. It'd be greatly appreciated!

Write me an honest review about the book – I truly value your opinion and thoughts and I will incorporate them into my next book, which is already underway.

Thank you!

If you have any questions, **feel free to contact at:** _author@rutabagarecipes.com_

Victoria Morgan

rutabagarecipes.com

Made in United States
Orlando, FL
20 November 2023